SRA

Corrective Reading

▶ # Comprehension Skills

Enrichment Blackline Masters   **Comprehension B1**

Siegfried Engelmann • Susan Hanner

SRA McGraw-Hill

Columbus, Ohio

A Division of The McGraw-Hill Companies

SRA/McGraw-Hill

*A Division of The **McGraw·Hill** Companies*

Printed in the United States of America.

Send all inquiries to:
SRA/McGraw-Hill
8787 Orion Place
Columbus, OH 43240-4027

ISBN 0-02-674808-8

7 8 9 0 MAL 05 04

Table of Contents

Part 1

Follow the directions.

1. Draw a horizontal line in the box.

2. Place a **b** under the left end of the line.

3. Write a **g** above the right end of the line.

Part 2

Read the sentence and answer the questions.

If he goes fishing, he will catch four fish.

1. What will happen if he goes fishing?

   _____

2. How many fish will he catch?

   _____

3. Who will get four fish?

   _____

4. What will he catch if he goes fishing?

   _____

☆ Part 3

Cross out the word that does not belong. The first one is done for you.

1. blue   white   red   ~~dog~~

2. milk   water   mud   juice

3. paper   book   frog   pencil

4. cat   run   jump   play

5. sad   angry   happy   cookie

6. Susie   Terry   Jim   elephant

7. dinner   breakfast   candle   lunch

8. game   doll   cry   ball

Following directions, making inferences, classifying
Directions: If necessary, read the directions for each part. When students have completed the page, present each item and the answer. Correct any errors.

1

Name _____

Part 4

Circle the part of the sentence that names.

1. David pushed a cart.

_____

2. Three tall girls skipped rope.

_____

3. Mom fixed the lawnmower.

_____

4. That cat climbs quickly.

_____

Part 5

Read the underlined word and the definitions. Fill in the circle next to the correct definition.

1. <u>obtain</u>   ○ cover   ○ get

2. <u>protect</u>   ○ guard   ○ teach

3. <u>examine</u>   ○ measure   ○ look at

4. <u>select</u>   ○ choose   ○ chew

Conventions of grammar/definitions
Directions: If necessary, read the directions for each part. When students have completed the page, present each item and the answer. Correct any errors.

Part 1

Circle the part of the sentence that names.

1. Jim ran very fast.

2. Mark typed his report.

3. The dog jumped on the couch.

4. Those five ducks quack loudly.

5. She ate her food.

Part 2

Read the sentence and answer the questions.

The skull sits at the top of the spine.

1. Where does the skull sit?

_____

2. Is the skull at the top of the spine?

_____

3. What is the skull at the top of?

_____

4. What is underneath the skull?

_____

☆ Part 3

Read the words in the box. Write each word in the correct group.

dance   red   eat   Andy   blue

green   Lupe   yellow   pink   Jenny

John   write   sing   talk   Dennis

Colors   **Names**   **Actions**

_____   _____   _____

_____   _____   _____

_____   _____   _____

_____   _____   _____

_____   _____   _____

Conventions of grammar, making inferences, classifying
Directions: If necessary, read the directions for each part. When students have completed the page, present each item and the answer. Correct any errors.

Part 4

Follow the directions.

1. Draw a horizontal line in the box.

2. Draw a slanted line under the right end of the horizontal line.

3. Draw a dot above the right end of the horizontal line.

Part 5

Fill in the circle next to the correct form of **obtain** for each of the following sentences.

1. They are _____ new toys.
   ○ obtain   ○ obtained   ○ obtaining

2. He _____ new toys.
   ○ obtain   ○ obtained   ○ obtaining

3. She will _____ new toys.
   ○ obtain   ○ obtained   ○ obtaining

4. I have _____ new toys.
   ○ obtain   ○ obtained   ○ obtaining

5. You are _____ new toys.
   ○ obtain   ○ obtained   ○ obtaining

Following directions, conventions of grammar
Directions: If necessary, read the directions for each part. When students have completed the page, present each item and the answer. Correct any errors.

Part 1

Read the sentence and answer the questions.

A large glass can hold lots of water.

1. What can hold lots of water?

   _____

2. What can a large glass hold?

   _____

3. How much water can a large glass hold?

   _____

4. What kind of glass can hold lots of water?

   _____

Part 2

Follow the directions.

1. Draw a horizontal line.

2. Draw a slanted line above the horizontal line.

3. Draw a vertical line over the slanted line.

Part 3

Circle the part of the sentence that names.

1. The man waved at a car.

2. Two boys waved at the cars.

3. Jane sat at a table.

4. My older brother stood next to my dad.

5. One boy is very happy.

6. A dog is an animal.

7. Dogs have tails.

8. Two large dogs herded the sheep.

☆ Part 4

Circle the thing that does not fit into each category below.

1. Things to play with

   games   dolls   stores   balls

2. Things to eat

   potatoes   lamps   carrots   apples

3. Parts of a bird

   hands   beak   head   wings

Making inferences, following directions, conventions of grammar, classifying
Directions: If necessary, read the directions for each part. When students have completed the page, present each item and the answer. Correct any errors.

Part 5

Circle each vehicle. Underline each container.

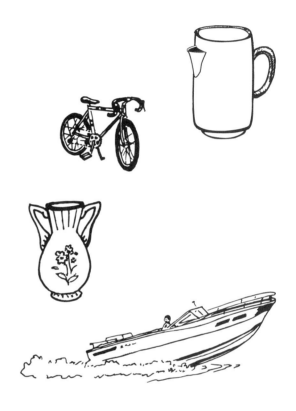
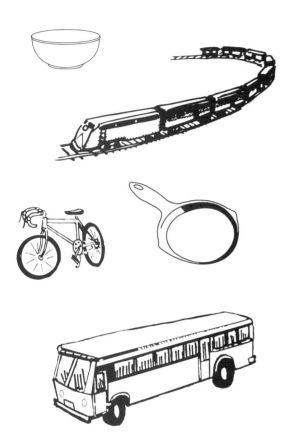

Classification
Directions: If necessary, read the directions for each part. When students have completed the page, present each item and the answer. Correct any errors.

☆ Part 1

Write the letter that comes next.

1. S   T   _____

2. E   F   _____

3. K   L   _____

4. J   K   _____

5. M   N   _____

Write the letter that comes in the middle.

6. E _____ G

7. C _____ E

8. L _____ N

9. S _____ U

10. W _____ Y

Write the letter that comes before.

11. _____ B   C

12. _____ L   M

13. _____ S   T

14. _____ F   G

15. _____ K   L

Part 2

Write the number of the fact that explains why each thing happened.

1. **Beth had a cat.**
2. **Beth had a hamster.**

a. Her pet had a scratching post. ____

b. Her pet had an exercise wheel. ____

c. Her pet was meowing. ____

d. Her pet lived in a cage. ____

Part 3

Follow the directions.

1. Draw a horizontal line in the box.

2. Draw a vertical line down from the right end of the horizontal line.

3. Draw a slanted line from the bottom of the vertical line to the left end of the horizontal line.

Alphabetical order, drawing conclusions based on evidence, following directions
Directions: If necessary, read the directions for each part. When students have completed the page, present each item and the answer. Correct any errors.

Part 4

Underline the part of the sentence that names.

1. That bus was moving very slowly.

2. A tired bird flew to a branch.

3. Tara got mad at Joey.

4. The wagon was blue.

5. The holiday lights look pretty at night.

6. My older brother has a new game.

7. Cats like to play with string.

8. The shiny new car hit a light pole.

Part 5

Underline each container.

Cross out each vehicle.

Conventions of grammar, classification
Directions: If necessary, read the directions for each part. When students have completed the page, present each item and the answer. Correct any errors.

☆ Part 1

Number the words in **ABC order.** Then write the words in the right order.

1. ____ ball   **1.** _____

    ____ apple   **2.** _____

    ____ car   **3.** _____

2. ____ dog   **1.** _____

    ____ fish   **2.** _____

    ____ egg   **3.** _____

3. ____ pan   **1.** _____

    ____ nail   **2.** _____

    ____ oak   **3.** _____

Part 2

Write a word that comes from **protect** in each blank.

1. The boy was _____ the fort.

2. That lock will _____ my locker.

3. Those gloves had _____ her hands.

4. Gary had a helmet to _____ his head.

Part 3

Write **ribs, skull,** or **spine** in each blank.

1. _____

2. _____

3. _____

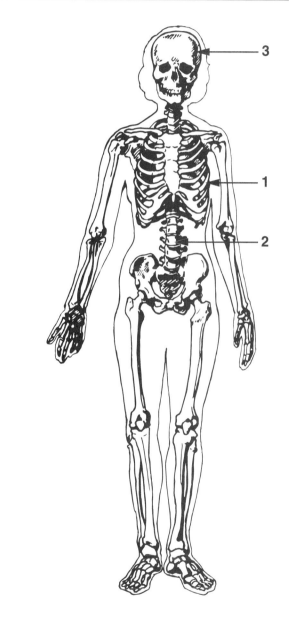

Alphabetical order, inflectional suffixes, graphic aids
Directions: If necessary, read the directions for each part. When students have completed the page, present each item and the answer. Correct any errors.

Part 4

Underline the part of each sentence that names.
Then circle the noun in that part.

1. The class lasted a short time.

2. My dad has a new suit.

3. That old white cat is very tired.

4. His mom worked very well.

5. That cat was a kitten.

6. Nigel wrote a fantastic story.

7. This grumpy baby frowns a lot.

8. Cars can't park in this space.

Part 5

Write the number of the fact that explains why
each thing happened.

1. The weather was wet.
2. The weather was dry.

a. The man slipped.   ____

b. The boy drank a lot of water.   ____

c. The woman wore a raincoat.   ____

d. They had a lot of trouble
   starting the campfire.   ____

Part 6

Follow the directions.

1. Draw a slanted line down to the left.

2. Draw a vertical line down from the top end
   of the slanted line.

3. Draw a slanted line from the bottom of the
   vertical line up to the right.

Conventions of grammar, drawing conclusions based on evidence, following directions
Directions: If necessary, read the directions for each part. When students have completed the page, present each item
and the answer. Correct any errors.

☆ Part 1

Write each set of words in **ABC order.**

| soap   dream   east |

1. _____
2. _____
3. _____

| trip   week   road |

1. _____
2. _____
3. _____

Part 2

Write a word that comes from **examine** in each blank.

1. A doctor will _____ my throat.

2. That dentist had _____ Tim's teeth.

3. Six policemen are _____ that old building.

4. This scientist wants to _____ Barbara's rock.

5. A baker will _____ this cake.

Part 3

Underline the part that names and circle the verb in each sentence.

1. Jake walked all day.

2. Her dad drove a new car.

3. Her dad was driving a new car.

4. Her dad was washing the car.

5. That girl painted a fence.

6. My mother was baking in the kitchen.

7. Robert went to the kitchen.

8. The dog slid across the floor.

Alphabetical order, inflectional suffixes, conventions of grammar
Directions: If necessary, read the directions for each part. When students have completed the page, present each item and the answer. Correct any errors.

Part 4

Write **ribs, skull,** or **spine** in each blank.

1. _____

2. _____

3. _____

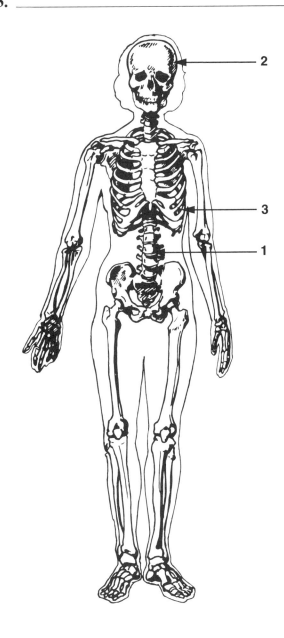

Part 5

Follow the directions.

1. Draw a horizontal line in the box.

2. Draw a vertical line down from the left end of the horizontal line.

3. Write a **7** on the right side of the vertical line.

Part 6

Read the sentence and answer the questions.

> **Those birds will make their nest in a tree or on a building ledge.**

1. Where will they make their nest?

_____

2. Will they make their nest in a tree and a building ledge?

_____

3. Will they make their nest in a tree or on a building ledge?

_____

4. What word tells whose nest the birds will make?

_____

Graphic aids, following directions, making inferences
Directions: If necessary, read the directions for each part. When students have completed the page, present each item and the answer. Correct any errors.

Part 1

Follow the directions.

1. Draw a vertical line in the box.

2. Draw a line that slants down to the left from the top of the vertical line.

3. Draw a line that slants down to the right from the top of the vertical line.

Part 2

Circle the word in each part that names. Make a box around the verb in each sentence.

1. The kids were producing a play.

2. The kids bought clothes for costumes.

3. Six girls were climbing that tree.

4. A white cat walked along the fence.

5. The boys swam in the creek.

6. My brother is swimming in the creek.

Part 3

Write the number of the fact that explains why each thing happened.

1. **Jessie has a sore hip.**
2. **Kelly broke her humerus.**

a. She has a cast on her arm. _____

b. A doctor examined her pelvis. _____

c. She has trouble going up stairs. _____

d. She has to write with her other hand. _____

Part 4

Write a word that comes from **obtain** in each blank.

1. She is _____ a piece of pie.

2. Eric wants to _____ a broom from this store.

3. He has _____ a football from this store.

4. They are _____ gold and silver from this mine.

5. Mac has _____ blue suspenders for his pants.

Following directions, conventions of grammar, drawing conclusions based on evidence, inflectional suffixes
Directions: If necessary, read the directions for each part. When students have completed the page, present each item and the answer. Correct any errors.

☆ Part 5

> Words that mean the same or nearly the same are called **synonyms**.
> **Examples:**
> sleep-rest   cold-chilly

Read each sentence below. Find a synonym from the box for each underlined word. Write the word on the line.

home	sick	small
dad	gift	yelled

1. Tim gave me a present for my birthday.

_____

2. I saw a little kitten in our yard.

_____

3. My house is on a corner.

_____

4. I almost fell ill.

_____

5. Dave shouted for me to go.

_____

6. My father travels a lot.

_____

Part 6

Write **humerus, femur,** or **pelvis** in each blank.

1. _____

2. _____

3. _____

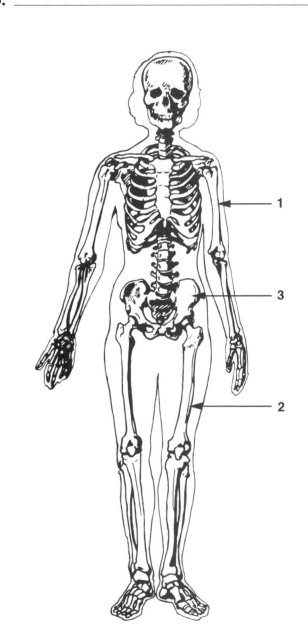

Synonyms, graphic aids
Directions: If necessary, read the directions for each part. When students have completed the page, present each item and the answer. Correct any errors.

Part 1

Underline the verbs.

1. A young girl protects her doll.

2. A woman protects the gold in that chest.

3. Her friend constructs chests and his pal selects games.

4. His friend constructs chests and selects games.

5. His little sister scuffed her shoe.

6. She cleaned off the scuff quickly.

☆ Part 2

Choose a synonym in ( ) for the underlined word.

1. The test was <u>simple</u>. (hard, easy)

   _____

2. Cody <u>likes</u> doing tricks. (hates, enjoys)

   _____

3. We watched the basketball player <u>jump</u> into the air. (leap, crawl)

   _____

4. The ladder is by the <u>back</u> door. (rear, front)

   _____

Part 3

Write **femur, humerus, pelvis, ribs, skull,** or **spine** in each blank.

1. _____

2. _____

3. _____

4. _____

5. _____

6. _____

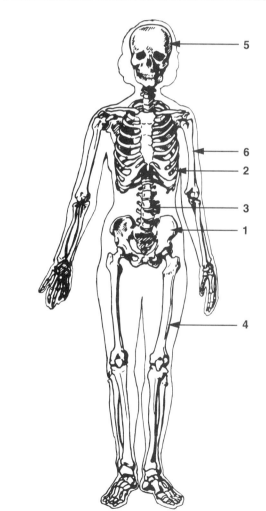

Conventions of grammar/verbs, synonyms, graphic aids
Directions: If necessary, read the directions for each part. When students have completed the page, present each item and the answer. Correct any errors.

Part 4

Write a word that comes from **construct** in each blank.

1. Mom wants to _____ a boat.

2. Those men are planning to _____ a house.

3. Her aunt is _____ a garage.

4. That boy has _____ a wooden scooter.

5. You cannot _____ a slide with sand.

Part 5

Write the number of the fact that explains why each thing happened.

1. **Warren was hot.**
2. **Gil was cold.**

a. He was sweating.   ___

b. He was fanning himself.   ___

c. He was shivering.   ___

d. He made hot chocolate.   ___

Part 6

Follow the directions.

1. Draw a vertical line in the box.

2. Draw two horizontal lines to the right of the vertical line.

3. Write a **q** at the bottom end of the vertical line.

Part 7

Circle the noun in each part. Underline the verb in each sentence.

1. Jan threw a football.

2. Many ducks were eating from the bird feeder.

3. His sister tripped on the curb.

4. Four small chipmunks were squeaking at Jim.

5. That girl eats lunch at noon.

6. Their father is building some stairs.

Inflectional suffixes, drawing conclusions based on evidence, following directions, conventions of grammar
Directions: If necessary, read the directions for each part. When students have completed the page, present each item and the answer. Correct any errors.

Part 1

For each numbered word, write the letter of the word's definition.

1. construct   _____   a. (v.) guard

2. examine   _____   b. (n.) the bone that covers the brain

3. obtain   _____   c. (n.) a word that tells the actions that things do

4. protect   _____   d. (v.) get

5. ribs   _____   e. (v.) choose

6. select   _____   f. (n.) the backbone

7. skeletal system _____ g. (v.) build

8. skull   _____   h. (n.) the bones that cover the organs in the chest

9. spine   _____   i. (v.) look at

10. verb   _____   j. (n.) the body system of bones

Part 2

Write the number of the fact that explains why each thing happened.

1. Joe said, "Buy."
2. Tom said, "Horse."

a. He said what to do.   ____

b. He said a verb.   ____

c. He said a noun.   ____

d. The thing he said was an animal. ____

Definitions, drawing conclusions based on evidence
Directions: If necessary, read the directions for each part. When students have completed the page, present each item and the answer. Correct any errors.

☆ Part 3

Use the words in the box below to write a synonym for each word.

road	cap	begin	hike
correct	happy	under	close

1. walk   _____

2. start   _____

3. glad   _____

4. hat   _____

5. shut   _____

6. below   _____

7. street   _____

8. right   _____

Part 4

Write a word that comes from **select** in each blank.

1. Nancy has _____ a dog for her family.

2. Scott will _____ a computer for his office.

3. Jon was _____ by the teacher.

4. The woman is _____ a skirt at the mall.

Part 5

Follow the directions.

1. Write a **Y** in the box.

2. Draw three horizontal lines to the right of the **Y**.

3. Write a **3** to the left of the **Y**.

Synonyms, inflectional suffixes, following directions
Directions: If necessary, read the directions for each part. When students have completed the page, present each item and the answer. Correct any errors.

Part 1

Underline both nouns in each sentence.

1. The boy ran from the park.

2. My father stood over that hole.

3. The woman drank the soda slowly.

4. David scanned the newspaper quickly.

5. My sister likes the circus.

6. Not many people live in Alaska.

Part 2

Read the sentence and answer the questions.

> **A carpenter has to construct lots of floors for new houses.**

1. Who has to construct floors?

   _____

2. What kind of houses does a carpenter construct floors for?

   _____

3. Does a carpenter build floors for houses?

   _____

4. How many floors does a carpenter construct?

   _____

☆ Part 3

> Words that mean the opposite are called **antonyms.**
> **Examples:**
> up-down   day-night

Draw a line to the antonym for each underlined word.

1. a high bridge   soft

2. a sad movie   dark

3. off the table   happy

4. a light color   long

5. a short story   on

6. a hard bed   low

Conventions of grammar, making inferences, antonyms
Directions: If necessary, read the directions for each part. When students have completed the page, present each item and the answer. Correct any errors.

Part 4

Write **skull, ribs, femur, humerus, spine,** or **pelvis** in each blank.

1. _____

2. _____

3. _____

4. _____

5. _____

6. _____

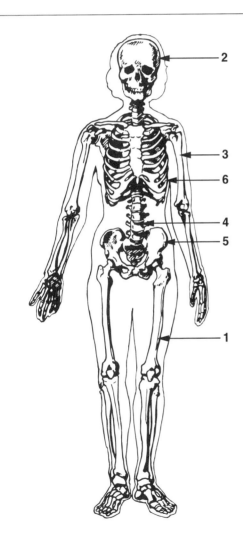

Part 5

Write a word that comes from **protect** in each blank.

1. The boot is _____ his foot.

2. That yard was _____ by a fence.

3. The police _____ you.

4. Your heart is _____ by your ribs.

5. The shack was _____ us from the rain.

Part 6

Circle the noun in each part. Underline the verb in each sentence.

1. The girl was running in the street.

2. The girls were running in the street.

3. The girls lived on a wide street.

4. This night is very cool.

5. Last night was cooler.

6. The grass feels cool.

Graphic aids, inflectional suffixes, conventions of grammar
Directions: If necessary, read the directions for each part. When students have completed the page, present each item and the answer. Correct any errors.

Part 1

Fill in each blank.

1. _____

2. _____

3. _____

4. _____

5. _____

6. _____

Part 2

Break the code. Fill in each blank. Then do what the sentence tells you to do.

| _____ | _____ | _____ |
| snay | q | cru |

| _____ | _____ | _____ |
| m | flep | ret |

q = a
flep = the
cru = circle
snay = make   _____
m = under
ret = line

Part 3

Underline each noun in the sentences. Circle each verb.

1. The train had a bent wheel.

2. His new hat was sitting on the table.

3. Joe sold old video games.

4. The young lion was running.

5. Our town constructed a new school.

6. Three girls and three boys played in the ocean.

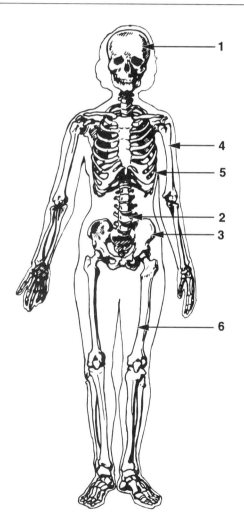

Graphic aids, following directions, conventions of grammar
Directions: If necessary, read the directions for each part. When students have completed the page, present each item and the answer. Correct any errors.

☆ Part 4

Choose an antonym in (   ) for the underlined word.

1. The student will answer either <u>yes</u> or

   _____.

   (maybe, no)

2. When food isn't <u>good</u>, it's

   _____.

   (hot, bad)

3. Summer is <u>hot</u>, and winter is

   _____.

   (snow, cold)

4. I like to run <u>fast</u>, not

   _____.

   (slow, far)

Part 5

Underline each noun in the sentences.

1. Marla doesn't like Tom as well as Matt.

2. A little girl walked on the couch.

3. My mom was washing the floor.

4. My brother kept his candy under his pillow.

5. Westin dropped a penny in the sewer.

Part 6

Read the sentence and answer the questions.

> **The woman cracked her femur when she tripped on the sidewalk.**

1. When did the woman crack her femur?

   _____

   _____

2. What bone did the woman break?

   _____

3. Where did the woman trip?

   _____

4. What did the woman do to her femur?

   _____

5. Who broke her femur?

   _____

Antonyms, conventions of grammar, making inferences
Directions: If necessary, read the directions for each part. When students have completed the page, present each item and the answer. Correct any errors.

Part 1

Break the code. Fill in each blank. Then do what the sentence tells you to do.

| _____ | _____ | _____ |
| jik | di | mij |

| _____ | _____ | _____ |
| nort | bac | fase |

jik = make
mij = box
fase = line
nort = over
bac = the
di = a

_____

Part 2

Write a word that comes from **construct** in each blank.

1. The farmers have _____ a large pig pen.

2. These toys were _____ by hand.

3. That deck was _____ by her dad.

4. Those wasps will _____ a hive.

5. The man is _____ a doghouse for his dog.

☆ Part 3

Read the words. Write **S** if the underlined words are synonyms. Write **A** if they are antonyms.

1. _____ old hat, new hat

2. _____ fast bike, quick bike

3. _____ large dog, big dog

4. _____ first day, last day

5. _____ cold drink, hot drink

Part 4

Circle each verb in the sentences.

1. The new car was running smoothly.

2. Some boys found a frog.

3. The cat purred and rolled over.

4. Don lost his balance and fell off the wall.

5. The man dug a ditch and sat on the edge.

6. Jill drank water and rubbed her arm.

7. Tony bought dinner and went home.

8. The clowns were chasing the dogs.

Following directions, inflectional suffixes, antonyms/synonyms, conventions of grammar
Directions: If necessary, read the directions for each part. When students have completed the page, present each item and the answer. Correct any errors.

Part 5

Circle each container.
Cross out each living thing.
Underline each piece of clothing.

Part 6

Fill in each blank.

1. _____

2. _____

3. _____

4. _____

5. _____

6. _____

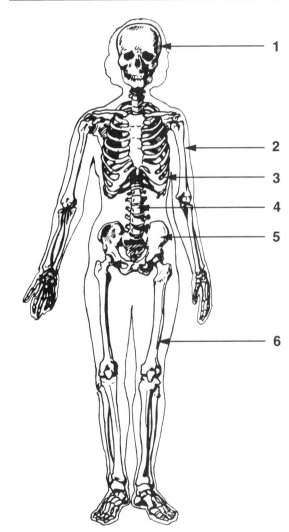

Classification, graphic aids
Directions: If necessary, read the directions for each part. When students have completed the page, present each item and the answer. Correct any errors.

LESSON 17

Name _____

Part 1

Break the code. Fill in each blank. Then do what the sentence tells you to do.

_____	_____	_____
falg	ga	berp

_____	_____	_____
por	h	diw

_____
xuh

ga = the
xuh = line
berp = word
por = femur
diw = the
falg = write
h = under

_____

Part 2

Write the number of the fact that explains why each thing happened.

1. **Jake fell out of a tree.**
2. **A doctor took care of Jake.**

a. His ankle was broken. ____

b. He lost his balance and fell. ____

c. He landed hard. ____

d. He put a cast on his foot. ____

Part 3

Fill in each blank.

1. _____

2. _____

3. _____

4. _____

5. _____

6. _____

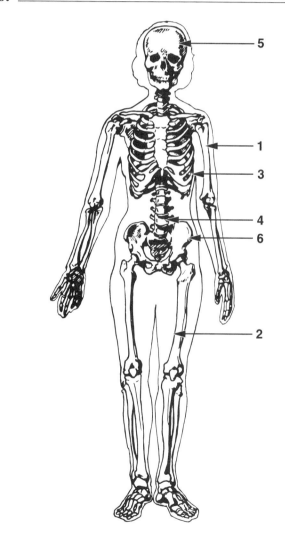

Following directions, draw conclusions based on evidence, graphic aids
Directions: If necessary, read the directions for each part. When students have completed the page, present each item and the answer. Correct any errors.

☆ Part 4

> Some sentences are statements. They tell something.
> *The Grand Canyon is in Arizona.*
>
> Some sentences are questions. They ask something.
> *Is the Grand Canyon in Arizona?*

Write **S** in front of each statement.
Write **Q** in front of each question.

_____ Sue ate fried chicken.

_____ Did Sarah find the rolls?

_____ Is he hungry?

_____ We walked to the park.

_____ Marcia left for her trip.

_____ Did he get sick and leave?

_____ Steve wanted to see the plane.

_____ Is Max ready to go?

_____ This was a long week.

_____ Will you give me one?

Part 5

Complete the deductions.

1. Every dog is a mammal.
   Roscoe is a dog.

   _____

2. All girls are persons.
   Gwen is a girl.

   _____

3. All of the Smiths are football fans.
   Terry's last name is Smith.

   _____

4. All birds have feathers.
   A penguin is a bird.

   _____

5. All nuts have a shell.
   A buckeye is a nut.

   _____

Types of sentences, deductions
Directions: If necessary, read the directions for each part. When students have completed the page, present each item and the answer. Correct any errors.

Part 1

Complete the deductions.

1. Kory has every video game.
   "Blitz" is a video game.

   _____

2. Andy likes all sweets.
   Bubble gum is sweet.

   _____

3. Fish can breathe under water.
   A trout is a fish.

   _____

4. Paper is made from tree pulp.
   You're writing on paper.

   _____

Part 2

Read the sentence in the box and answer the questions.

Dogs eat meat and deer eat plants.

1. Which kind of animal eats meat?

   _____

2. Which kind of animal eats plants?

   _____

3. Do deer eat meat and plants?

   _____

4. What do dogs eat?

   _____

5. Do dogs eat meat and plants?

   _____

☆ Part 3

> Some sentences are commands. They tell somebody to do something.
> *Please set the table.*
>
> Some sentences are exclamations. They show strong feelings or surprise.
> *What a wonderful trip!*

Write **C** in front of each command.
Write **E** in front of each exclamation.

_____   What a great time we'll have!

_____   Add the eggs to the batter.

_____   Watch out for that ladder.

_____   Brush your teeth first.

_____   The dog ate the hamburger!

_____   I am so happy!

_____   Pass the salt, please.

_____   Clean the sink well.

_____   Slice the apples.

_____   What a cute puppy!

Deductions, making inferences, types of sentences
Directions: If necessary, read the directions for each part. When students have completed the page, present each item and the answer. Correct any errors.

Part 5

For each numbered word, write the letter of the word's definition.

1. construct _____   a. (v.) choose

2. examine _____   b. (v.) get

3. femur _____   c. (v.) build

4. humerus _____   d. (n.) the upper arm bone

5. noun _____   e. (n.) the hip bone

6. obtain _____   f. (v.) look at

7. pelvis _____   g. (v.) guard

8. protect _____   h. (n.) a word that names a person, place, or thing

9. select _____   i. (n.) the upper leg bone

10. verb _____   j. (n.) a word that tells the action that things do

Definitions
Directions: If necessary, read the directions for each part. When students have completed the page, present each item and the answer. Correct any errors.

☆ Part 1

> Put a period (.) at the end of a statement.
> *Pat is my friend.*
>
> Put a question mark (?) at the end of a question.
> *Where did she go?*
>
> Put an exclamation mark (!) at the end of an exclamation.
> *Watch out!*
>
> Put a period (.) at the end of a command.
> *Turn off the water.*

Read each sentence and put the correct punctuation mark at the end.

1. We are in school today____

2. He has a younger sister____

3. It's snowing really hard____

4. Is that your bike____

5. It's so cold today____

6. Let's walk to the movie____

Part 2

Write a word that comes from **protect** in each blank. Then fill in the circle next to **verb, noun,** or **adjective.**

1. The _____ dog scared the intruder.
○ verb   ○ noun   ○ adjective

2. The cheetah had to _____ her cubs.
○ verb   ○ noun   ○ adjective

3. Insurance policies provide _____ against loss from theft, fire, and floods.
○ verb   ○ noun   ○ adjective

Part 3

Write the number of the fact that explains why each thing happened.

1. Lonnie got an old rookie baseball card.
2. Sam found a green rock.

a. It cost him a lot.   ___

b. He will show it to his science class.   ___

c. He will keep it in a special folder.   ___

d. He is careful not to drop it on his foot.   ___

Types of sentences, inflectional suffixes, drawing conclusions based on evidence
Directions: If necessary, read the directions for each part. When students have completed the page, present each item and the answer. Correct any errors.

Part 4

Follow the directions.

1. Draw a horizontal line from the left side of the box to the right side of the box.

2. Draw a circle underneath the horizontal line.

3. Draw three vertical lines above the horizontal line.

Part 5

Complete the deductions.

1. Jon does not have anything made of leather.
   Baseball gloves are made of leather.

   _____

   _____

2. Teachers are smart people.
   Megan is a teacher.

   _____

   _____

Part 6

Circle the verbs. Underline the nouns.

1. Broken glass is not safe.

2. Mom is going to a recital.

3. The man baked pies.

4. Barb welded pipes and drove nails.

5. Seth and John love their pool.

6. Lee knew Kay's aunt and uncle.

Following directions, deductions, conventions of grammar
Directions: If necessary, read the directions for each part. When students have completed the page, present each item and the answer. Correct any errors.

Part 1

Read the story and answer the questions.

> Kelvin's back hurt, so he went to a doctor. The doctor said, "You've been lifting lots and lots of heavy boxes. If you don't take a break, you could hurt your back forever."

1. Why did Kelvin go to a doctor?

_____

2. How many boxes did Kelvin lift?

_____

3. What will happen if Kelvin doesn't take a break?

_____

4. How could Kelvin hurt his back forever?

_____

☆ Part 2

> Names of the days of the week begin with a capital letter.
> **Examples:** Sunday, Monday, Friday
>
> Abbreviations of the days of the week begin with a capital letter.
> **Examples:** Sun., Mon., Tues., Wed., Thurs., Fri., Sat.

Write the days of the week to complete each sentence.

1. The first day of the week is

_____

2. The day that comes before Sunday is

_____

3. The day in the middle of the week is

_____

Write the correct abbreviation for the day of the week.

Sunday   _____

Monday   _____

Tuesday   _____

Wednesday   _____

Thursday   _____

Friday   _____

Saturday   _____

Making inferences, following directions, capitalization
Directions: If necessary, read the directions for each part. When students have completed the page, present each item and the answer. Correct any errors.

Part 3

Complete the analogy by filling in the circle next to the best choice.

A **monkey** is to **climbing**

1. as a dolphin is to _____.
   ○ crawling
   ○ swimming

2. as a kangaroo is to _____.
   ○ running
   ○ hopping

3. as a tiger is to _____.
   ○ swimming
   ○ running

Part 4

Complete the deductions.

1. Fred did not have any pets.
   A hamster is a pet.

   _____

   _____

2. An adjective is a word that describes something.
   Interesting is an adjective.

   _____

   _____

Part 5

Write the number of the fact that explains why each thing happened.

1. **Kyle said, "Obtain."**
2. **Tom said, "Construction."**

a. He said a verb.   ____

b. He said a noun.   ____

c. He was talking about something that is built.   ____

d. He was talking about getting something.   ____

Part 6

Draw a line over each adjective.

1. Many fish need salt water.

2. Big cars are hard to drive.

3. The bright sun helped the plants grow.

4. Small dogs bark more than big dogs.

5. My sister is a very pretty girl.

6. Jasper, where is your green shirt?

Analogies, deductions, drawing conclusions based on evidence, conventions of grammar
Directions: If necessary, read the directions for each part. When students have completed the page, present each item and the answer. Correct any errors.

Part 1

Write **esophagus, mouth,** or **stomach** in each blank.

1. _____

2. _____

3. _____

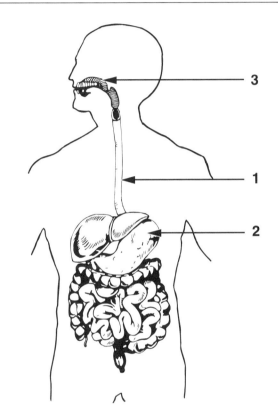

Part 2

Fill in each blank with the word that has the same meaning as the word or words under the blank.

examine	protecting
select	constructed

1. He told her to _____ six problems.   (look at)

2. Those dogs are _____ that house.   (guarding)

3. The boy was allowed to _____ one puppy.   (choose)

4. Who _____ that tree house? (built)

Part 3

Complete the analogy by filling in the circle next to the best choice.

A **tongue** is to **tasting**

1. as **feet** are to _____.
   ○ hearing   ○ seeing   ○ running

2. as **eyes** are to _____.
   ○ hearing   ○ seeing   ○ running

3. as **ears** are to _____.
   ○ hearing   ○ seeing   ○ running

Graphic aids, vocabulary, analogies
Directions: If necessary, read the directions for each part. When students have completed the page, present each item and the answer. Correct any errors.

Part 4

Circle the verbs. Underline the nouns.

1. That dog was standing on the rug.

2. Those women were lawyers.

3. His dog has eaten.

4. That cop is a woman.

5. Four cats are on the fence.

6. Those boys were playing.

Part 5

Fill in each blank. Then do what the sentence tells you to do.

_____	_____	_____
graz	pulg	pim

_____	_____	_____
dok	kur	gurb

_____
dilk

pulg = a
kur = over
graz = make
gurb = the
dilk = K
pim = horizontal
dok = line

☆ Part 6

> - Names of the months begin with a capital letter.
> - The abbreviations of the months end with a period.
>   **Examples:** **J**an., **F**eb., **M**ar., **D**ec.

Write the names of the months correctly.

1. january _____

2. february _____

3. march _____

4. april _____

5. may _____

6. june _____

7. july _____

8. august _____

9. september _____

10. october _____

11. november _____

12. december _____

Conventions of grammar, following directions, capitalization
Directions: If necessary, read the directions for each part. When students have completed the page, present each item and the answer. Correct any errors.

☆ Part 1

> • Each word in the name of a holiday begins with a **capital letter.**
> **Examples:**
> Memorial **D**ay Labor **D**ay

Write the holiday names correctly.

1. new year's day

_____

2. thanksgiving day

_____

3. independence day

_____

4. valentine's day

_____

5. father's day

_____

6. martin luther king, jr. day

_____

Part 2

Complete the analogy.

Examine is to **look** at

1. as **select** is to _____.

2. as **protect** is to _____.

3. as **obtain** is to _____.

Part 3

Use the words in the box to complete the sentences.

constructed	obtained
protect	selecting

1. Their security system was selected to

_____ that house.
     (guard)

2. A fisherman _____ some
lobster traps.   (built)

3. He _____ some tools for his
brother.   (got)

4. They are _____ a school for him
to attend.   (choosing)

Capitalization, conventions of grammar/verbs, analogies, vocabulary
Directions: If necessary, read the directions for each part. When students have completed the page, present each item and the answer. Correct any errors.

Part 4

Write **mouth, esophagus,** or **stomach** in each blank.

1. _____

2. _____

3. _____

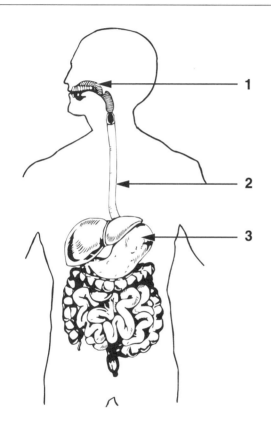

Part 5

Read the story and answer the questions.

> Zach wanted to clean his clothes, so he threw them over a clothesline in the backyard. "You can't wash your clothes on a clothesline," his dad said, "but you can dry them on the line after you wash them." So Zach washed his clothes in the sink, then hung them on the clothesline to dry.

1. Did Zach use the sink at first?

   _____

2. When did Zach use the sink?

   _____

   _____

3. When can you use a clothesline?

   _____

   _____

4. Did Zach wash or dry the clothes first?

   _____

5. Who told Zach he couldn't use the

   clothesline first? _____

Graphic aids, making inferences
Directions: If necessary, read the directions for each part. When students have completed the page, present each item and the answer. Correct any errors.

Part 1

For each numbered word or phrase write the letter of its definition.

1. adjective   _____   a. (n.) something that protects

2. construct   _____   b. (n.) a word that comes before a noun and tells about the noun

3. digestive system   _____   c. (v.) choose

4. esophagus   _____   d. (v.) build

5. mouth   _____   e. (v.) get

6. obtain   _____   f. (n.) the organ that mixes food with chemicals

7. protection   _____   g. (a.) that something protects

8. protective   _____   h. (n.) the body system that changes food into fuel

9. select   _____   i. (n.) the tube that goes from the mouth to the stomach

10. stomach   _____   j. (n.) the part that takes in solid and liquid food

Part 2

Follow the directions.

1. Draw a horizontal line.

2. Draw a line that slants down to the left from the left end of the horizontal line.

3. Draw a line from the bottom of the slanted line to the right end of the horizontal line.

Definitions, following directions
Directions: If necessary, read the directions for each part. When students have completed the page, present each item and the answer. Correct any errors.

Part 3

Read the story and answer the questions.

> It was snowing, and Jenny wanted to use her new sled. She took her sled to her backyard and sat down on it, but the sled didn't move. Her mom said, "You need a steep hill. The steeper the hill, the better the sled will slide."

1. What did Jenny want to use?

_____

2. What will happen if Jenny finds a steeper hill?

_____

_____

3. Will the sled slide better on a steep hill or in a flat yard?

_____

_____

4. What kind of hill will make the sled slide?

_____

5. If Jenny finds a steep hill, what will the sled do?

_____

_____

☆ Part 4

> - A **contraction** is a word made by joining two words.
> - An **apostrophe** (') shows where a letter or letters are left out.
> Examples:
> do not = don't   is not = isn't
> can not = can't   are not = aren't

Draw a line from the two words to the contraction.

1. was not   hasn't

2. were not   didn't

3. did not   aren't

4. has not   haven't

5. are not   weren't

6. have not   wasn't

Write each contraction as two words.

7. don't   _____ _____

8. can't   _____ _____

9. hadn't   _____ _____

10. isn't   _____ _____

Making inferences, contractions
Directions: If necessary, read the directions for each part. When students have completed the page, present each item and the answer. Correct any errors.

Part 1

Underline the nouns. Draw a line over the adjectives.

1. His friend ate on the dock.

2. The woman rode her bike down trails.

3. A rap group will play in our city.

4. A blue envelope is in the doorway.

5. Her mom and her brother were sitting on rocks.

6. That truck is in a narrow alley.

7. Two sharks ate fast fish and green eels.

8. Her father read in the shaded hammock.

Part 2

Complete the analogy.

A **spine** is to a **back**

1. as a **pelvis** is to a _____.

2. as a **femur** is to a _____.

3. as a **humerus** is to an _____.

Part 3

Write **small intestine, large intestine,** or **liver** in each blank.

1. _____

2. _____

3. _____

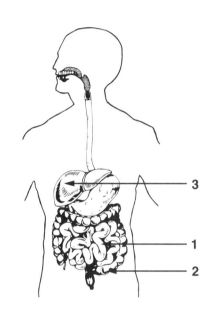

Conventions of grammar, analogies, graphic aids

Directions: If necessary, read the directions for each part. When students have completed the page, present each item and the answer. Correct any errors.

Part 4

Read the story and answer the questions.

> A young boy liked candy more than fruit. His doctor told him, "Candy is bad for your digestive system. You should eat fruit. The more fruit you eat, the better you will feel." So the young boy ate fruit, but he would reward himself with candy when he got good grades in school.

1. What did the young boy like more than fruit?

   _____

2. What did the doctor tell him to eat?

   _____

3. What will happen if the boy eats more fruit?

   _____

4. When did he eat candy? _____

   _____

5. If he wants to feel better, what will he do?

   _____

   _____

☆ Part 5

Underline each contraction.

1. Let's eat something now.

2. They can't see everything.

3. We'll wait outside for you.

4. Doesn't it seem like spring today?

5. I wish he wasn't going to the city.

Part 6

Follow the directions.

1. Draw a vertical line.

2. Write a **J** at the top end of the vertical line.

3. Write a **K** at the bottom end of the vertical line.

4. Write a **D** to the left of the vertical line.

Making inferences, contractions, following directions
Directions: If necessary, read the directions for each part. When students have completed the page, present each item and the answer. Correct any errors.

Name _____

Part 1

Write **stomach, mouth, liver, esophagus, large intestine,** or **small intestine** in each blank.

1. _____

2. _____

3. _____

4. _____

5. _____

6. _____

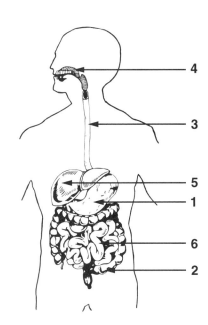

Part 2

Write a word that comes from **obtain** or **construct** in each blank. Then fill in the circle next to **verb, noun,** or **adjective**.

1. An old man will _____ a pair of slippers from the store.
   ○ verb   ○ noun   ○ adjective

2. Those _____ twins make the most of their time.
   ○ verb   ○ noun   ○ adjective

3. There will be a lot of _____ downtown this summer.
   ○ verb   ○ noun   ○ adjective

4. I'll bet he _____ those diamonds illegally.
   ○ verb   ○ noun   ○ adjective

5. The _____ will be off-limits to children.
   ○ verb   ○ noun   ○ adjective

Part 3

Complete the analogy.

A **noun** is to **parts of speech**

1. as a **lion** is to _____.

2. as a **bus** is to _____.

3. as a **fern** is to _____.

Graphic aids, conventions of grammar, analogies
Directions: If necessary, read the directions for each part. When students have completed the page, present each item and the answer. Correct any errors.

Part 4

Read the sentences and answer the questions. Circle **W** after each question that is answered by words in the sentences, and underline those words. Circle **D** after each question that is answered by a deduction.

1. **Every person has a stomach.**
2. **Carla is a person.**

a. What does every person have?

   _____ **W D**

b. Does Carla have a stomach?

   _____ **W D**

c. Does Carla have a digestive system?

   _____ **W D**

d. Is Carla a person? _____ **W D**

Part 5

Circle the verbs. Underline the nouns.

1. A small man cut flowers.

2. Four pandas live at the animal refuge.

3. Her dad is an engineer.

4. Many people enjoy baseball and football.

☆ Part 6

Write a **contraction** for the two words in parentheses.

1. I (do not)_____ have my lunch today.

2. My friends (were not)_____ in the gym.

3. Mary (is not) _____ planning on going to camp.

4. (Did not) _____ you put the dog out this morning?

5. Her parents (are not)_____ moving.

6. I (can not) _____ figure out this problem.

7. Jane and Tracy (have not) _____been to New York City.

Deductions, conventions of grammar, contractions
Directions: If necessary, read the directions for each part. When students have completed the page, present each item and the answer. Correct any errors.

Part 1

Make each sentence begin with a capital letter. Put the correct punctuation mark at the end of each sentence.

1. i'm very excited that my grandparents are coming_____

2. i'd like to examine your baseball card collection_____

3. tony enjoyed throwing darts with Pete_____

4. could you help me with this math problem_____

5. has anyone seen my shoes_____

Part 2

Fill in each blank. Then do what the sentence tells you to do.

67	98	45

32	54

45 = the
54 = oval
67 = shade
98 = in
32 = right

Part 3

Read the sentences and answer the questions. Circle **W** after each question that is answered by words in the sentences, and underline those words. Circle **D** after each question that is answered by a deduction.

Some words are adjectives.
Snappy **is a word.**

1. Is **snappy** an adjective?

   _____ **W D**

2. What are some words?

   _____ **W D**

3. How many words are adjectives?

   _____ **W D**

4. Does **snappy** describe a noun?

   _____ **W D**

Part 4

Underline the nouns. Draw a line over the adjectives. Circle the verbs.

1. Those two men cut four small trees.

2. Kathy and her sister enjoy fishing with their mom.

3. Skiing is a fun activity.

Capitalization/punctuation, following directions, deductions, conventions of grammar
Directions: If necessary, read the directions for each part. When students have completed the page, present each item and the answer. Correct any errors.

Part 5

Write a word that comes from **examine** or **select** in each blank. Then fill in the circle next to **verb, noun,** or **adjective.**

1. A nurse will _____ Kristi's feet.
   ○ verb   ○ noun   ○ adjective

2. James is a very _____ person.
   ○ verb   ○ noun   ○ adjective

3. The teacher _____ three students to do problems on the board.
   ○ verb   ○ noun   ○ adjective

4. Frank's _____ of video games is enormous.
   ○ verb   ○ noun   ○ adjective

Part 6

Underline the common part. Then combine the sentences with **and.**

1. Sal had nuts.
   Sal had bolts.

   _____

2. Joanna went to the park.
   Joanna picked four daisies.

   _____

   _____

☆Part 7

> • A **compound word** is made by joining one word with another word.
>
> Example: rain + bow = rainbow

Write the compound word made by joining each pair of words.

1. bath   +   tub   =   _____

2. fire   +   place   =   _____

3. sun   +   set   =   _____

4. sail   +   boat   =   _____

5. cat   +   fish   =   _____

6. down   +   stairs   =   _____

7. birth   +   day   =   _____

8. snow   +   ball   =   _____

Inflectional suffixes, conjunctions, compound words
Directions: If necessary, read the directions for each part. When students have completed the page, present each item and the answer. Correct any errors.

Part 1

Read the story and answer the questions.

> Terry got home from school and was
> excited about getting in his boat and sailing
> on the pond. However, when he got to the
> pond, he found it was completely frozen.
> Terry's brother, Wayne, was covering their
> boat with a tarp. "We can't sail until it
> warms up, Terry," Wayne said. "Boats
> won't float on ice. Of course, they won't
> sink, either, but we can't use our boat again
> until the spring."

1. Can the boat float on ice? _____

2. Can the boat sink in ice? _____

3. When can Terry sail again?

_____

4. Why was Wayne covering the boat with a

tarp? _____

_____

5. In what season do you think this happened?

_____

_____

Part 2

Write **large intestine, esophagus, mouth, liver,
stomach,** or **small intestine** in each blank.

1. _____

2. _____

3. _____

4. _____

5. _____

6. _____

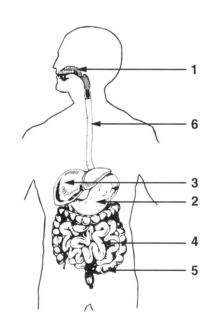

Deductions, graphic aids
Directions: If necessary, read the directions for each part. When students have completed the page, present each item
and the answer. Correct any errors.

Part 3

Underline the common part. Then combine the sentences with **and.**

1. Omar liked to play football.
   Omar liked to read books.

   _____

   _____

2. The roller rink offered a deal.
   The roller rink had lots of customers.

   _____

   _____

3. Tanya made popcorn.
   Tanya rented a video.

   _____

   _____

4. The dog ate the shoe.
   The dog buried the bone.

   _____

   _____

5. His dad bought two tomato cages.
   His dad bought a hoe.

   _____

   _____

☆ Part 4

Write the **compound word** from the box below that best completes the sentence.

newspaper	football	pancakes
seashell	raincoat	classmate

1. Do I have time to read the _____?

2. On Saturday we always have

   _____ for breakfast.

3. Please wear your _____ because it is raining.

4. My _____ let me borrow a piece of paper.

5. We found the prettiest _____ at the beach!

Part 5

Make each sentence begin with a capital letter. Put the correct punctuation mark at the end of each sentence.

1. where does this glass belong_____

2. all that chalk is red_____

3. her friend stood over the crack_____

4. who is going to be there_____

5. can you ride a bike_____

Conjunctions, compound words, capitalization/punctuation
Directions: If necessary, read the directions for each part. When students have completed the page, present each item and the answer. Correct any errors.

Part 1

For each numbered word, write the letter of the word's definition.

1. adjective   _____   a.   (n.) a word that tells the action that things do

2. examine   _____   b.   (n.) a word that names a person, place, or thing

3. large intestine   _____   c.   (n.) something that is selected

4. liver   _____   d.   (n.) the organ that gives food to the blood

5. noun   _____   e.   (n.) a word that comes before a noun and tells about the noun

6. protect   _____   f.   (v.) choose

7. select   _____   g.   (v.) look at

8. selection   _____   h.   (n.) organ that makes chemicals that break down food

9. small intestine   _____   i.   (v.) guard

10. verb   _____   j.   (n.) the organ that stores food the body cannot use

Definitions
Directions: If necessary, read the directions for each part. When students have completed the page, present each item and the answer. Correct any errors.

Part 2

Read the story and answer the questions.

> Terry waited for spring. When it was nice and warm, he and Wayne went down to the pond. The ice had melted, so they uncovered their boat and pushed it into the water. As they were preparing to board their boat, it began to sink. Terry said, "Our boat's sinking!"
>
> Wayne said, "Well, that just proves that this is water. Boats sink in water, not in ice."

1. Why did Terry wait for spring to put the boat into the pond?

_____

_____

2. What happened after Wayne and Terry pushed their boat into the water?

_____

_____

3. Would the boat have sunk in the ice?

_____

Part 3

Follow the directions.

1. Draw a square.

2. Draw a line from the lower left corner of the square to the upper right corner of the square.

3. Shade the area to the bottom right of the line.

☆ Part 4

Underline the **compound word** in each sentence. Then, write the two words that form the compound word.

1. The classroom had new desks.

_____ _____

2. We went to the seashore for a vacation.

_____ _____

3. The snowflake landed on my mitten.

_____ _____

4. My sweatshirt is in the wash.

_____ _____

Making inferences, following directions, compound words
Directions: If necessary, read the directions for each part. When students have completed the page, present each item and the answer. Correct any errors.

Part 1

Underline the common part. Then combine the sentences with **and.**

1. Coal is black.
Ink is black.

_____

_____

2. Two pans were on the stove.
Two pots were on the stove.

_____

_____

3. Dogs eat meat.
Lions eat meat.

_____

_____

4. Trey bumped his knee.
Trey cut his finger.

_____

_____

5. A company constructed a building.
A company constructed a dam.

_____

_____

6. Greg wanted to see the movie.
Vicky wanted to see the movie.

_____

_____

☆ Part 2

> • Words that sound the same but are
> spelled differently are called
> **homophones.**
> **Examples: sun/son so/sew blue/blew**

Use the homophones in the box to complete the sentences below.

sea see	sail sale	won one

1. The shoe _____ was last weekend.

2. I want to _____ to the island.

3. I can _____ that you have not finished your dinner.

4. The _____ is calm this morning.

5. I _____ a blue ribbon at the fair.

6. This is the _____ I want to keep.

Part 3

Follow the directions.

1. Draw a big circle.

2. Draw a slanted line from the top left of the circle to the bottom right of the circle.

3. Draw a vertical line from the top of the circle to the center of the slanted line.

4. Shade in the smallest part.

Conjunctions, homophones, following directions
Directions: If necessary, read the directions for each part. When students have completed the page, present each item and the answer. Correct any errors.

Name _____

Part 4

Fill in each blank.

1. _____

2. _____

3. _____

4. _____

5. _____

6. _____

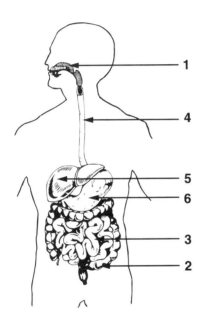

Part 5

Use the rule to answer the questions.

> The drier the air, the farther a baseball will travel.

1. Baseballs travel farther in summer air than in winter air.

   a. Which air is more humid?

   _____

   b. How do you know?

   _____

   _____

2. The air in Atlanta is more humid than the air in San Diego.

   a. In which city do baseballs travel farther?

   _____

   b. How do you know?

   _____

   _____

Graphic aids, making inferences
Directions: If necessary, read the directions for each part. When students have completed the page, present each item and the answer. Correct any errors.

50

LESSON 30

Name _____

☆ Part 1

Use the **homophones** in the box to complete the sentences below.

here	hear	write	right	ate	eight
for	four	way	weigh	new	knew

Use the homophones in the box to complete the sentences below.

1. Did you _____ the fire alarm?

2. Please put your library book

   _____.

3. I think I _____ the answer.

4. Our _____ car is a station wagon.

5. Please wait _____ me.

6. Did she have _____ sisters?

7. I _____ with my left hand.

8. Turn _____ at the stop sign.

9. I will _____ the potatoes.

10. Did you say to go this _____?

11. I _____ a piece of toast for breakfast.

12. There are _____ boys in our class.

Part 2

Complete the instructions.

pelvis ① _____
②   femur
                            ③

1. Draw two _____ lines.

2. Write the word _____ at the

   _____ end of the lower line.

3. Write the word _____ below the

   _____ end of the lower line.

Homophones, following directions
Directions: If necessary, read the directions for each part. When students have completed the page, present each item and the answer. Correct any errors.

Part 3

Fill in each blank with the word that has the same meaning as the word or words below the blank.

1. Many monkeys _____
(look at)
each other for ticks and mites.

2. The director _____ an
(chose)
actor for her play.

3. That boy is _____ a
(building)
soapbox racer.

4. Luke _____ the video
(got)
game he wanted.

Part 4

Complete the analogies.

1. Tell what class each thing is in.

A **car** is to _____

as a **box** is to _____.

2. Tell what each thing is made of.

A **car** is to _____

as a **box** is to _____.

3. Tell what each thing is made to do.

A **car** is to _____

as a **box** is to _____.

Part 5

Use the rule to answer the questions.

> **If you don't get enough iron in your diet, you can get tired easily.**

1. Bailey doesn't get enough iron in his diet.
a. What happens to Bailey?

_____

b. How do you know?

_____

_____

2. Peg never gets tired.
a. What do you know about Peg?

_____

b. How do you know?

_____

_____

3. Mark takes vitamins that contain iron.
Frank never takes any vitamins.
a. Which person is more likely to get tired?

_____

b. How do you know?

_____

_____

Vocabulary, analogies, making inferences
Directions: If necessary, read the directions for each part. When students have completed the page, present each item and the answer. Correct any errors.

☆Part 1

Read each sentence. Draw a line through the **homophone** that is used incorrectly. Then write the correct word in the blank.

1. We went in the knew car. _____

2. I have for dollars in my pocket.
_____

3. We eight dinner at six o'clock. _____

4. The wind blue my hat off. _____

5. I want to get the write answer. _____

6. We were all scent home. _____

7. The coat sail was in August. _____

8. I like to wear my hare in pigtails.

_____

Part 2

Fill in each blank.

1. _____

2. _____

3. _____

4. _____

5. _____

6. _____

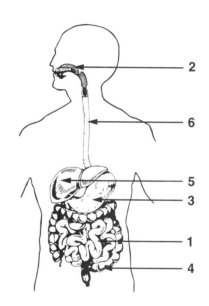

Homophones, graphic aids
Directions: If necessary, read the directions for each part. When students have completed the page, present each item and the answer. Correct any errors.

53

Part 3

Underline the nouns. Draw a line over the adjectives. Circle the verbs.

1. My friend constructs rocking horses.

2. Those men are constructing houses.

3. Boys and girls watched the construction.

4. His friends play near the construction.

5. Builders constructed that church.

Part 4

Complete the instructions.

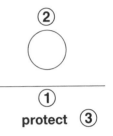

1. Draw a _____ line.

2. Draw a _____ above the

   _____ line.

3. Write the word _____ under the

   _____ line.

Part 5

Use the rule to answer the questions.

> You get a disease called scurvy if you don't get any vitamin C.

1. Janice doesn't get any vitamin C.
   a. What will happen to Janice?

   _____

   _____

   b. How do you know?

   _____

   _____

2. Chris got scurvy.
   a. What else do you know about Chris?

   _____

   b. How do you know?

   _____

3. Matt eats oranges, which have lots of vitamin C. Francis never eats oranges or any other foods with vitamin C.
   a. Which person well get scurvy?

   _____

   b. How do you know?

   _____

   _____

Conventions of grammar, following directions, making inferences
Directions: If necessary, read the directions for each part. When students have completed the page, present each item and the answer. Correct any errors.

Part 1

Write a word that comes from **obtain** or **construct** in each blank. Fill in the correct circle next to **verb, noun,** or **adjective.**

1. A carpenter is _____ a ship with a hammer.
   ○ verb   ○ noun   ○ adjective

2. The _____ of that road will take eight years.
   ○ verb   ○ noun   ○ adjective

3. Lori will _____ several dogs from the pound.
   ○ verb   ○ noun   ○ adjective

☆ Part 2

> • An **adjective** is a word that describes a noun. It tells *which one, how many,* or *what kind.*
> Example: **The two** dogs made **a loud** noise.

Underline the adjectives.

1. The big deer ran back into the woods.

2. Martin ate two bites of his sandwich.

3. The noisy car stopped at the corner.

4. My older sister wanted to go to the prom.

5. We walked inside the new house.

6. Dancing is good exercise.

7. Jenny asked for five dollars for the mall.

8. Isn't the new grocery store open?

9. Chocolate milkshakes are my favorite.

10. Your new puppy likes to eat socks.

Inflectional suffixes, adjectives
Directions: If necessary, read the directions for each part. When students have completed the page, present each item and the answer. Correct any errors.

Part 3

Fill in each blank.

1. _____

2. _____

3. _____

4. _____

5. _____

6. _____

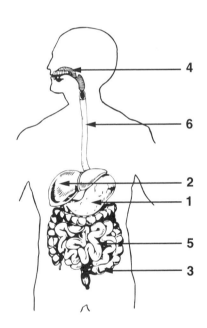

Part 4

Underline the common part. Then combine the sentences with **and.**

1. Asa cleans the house for fun.
   Rachel cleans the house for fun.

   _____

   _____

2. A dolphin swims in the ocean.
   A marlin swims in the ocean.

   _____

   _____

3. Nick obtained oil.
   Nick oiled his bike chain.

   _____

   _____

4. This rabbit burrows in cedar chips.
   That rabbit burrows in cedar chips.

   _____

   _____

5. Carly grows beans.
   Carly kills weeds.

   _____

   _____

Graphic aids, conjunctions
Directions: If necessary, read the directions for each part. When students have completed the page, present each item and the answer. Correct any errors.

LESSON 33

Name _____

Part 1

Write **quadriceps, biceps,** or **abdominal muscle** in each blank.

1. _____

2. _____

3. _____

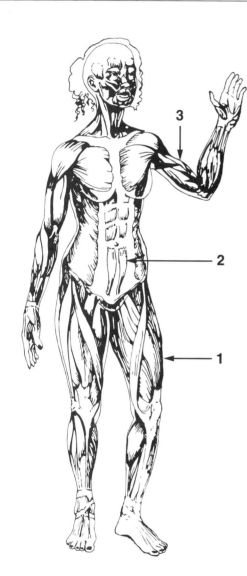

☆ Part 2

Complete the sentences with adjectives from the box.

happy two huge clean

1. Your _____ clothes are in the basket.

2. The _____ cloud looked like rain.

3. I have _____ days to get ready for the trip.

4. The _____ baby smiled at me.

Part 3

Complete the instructions.

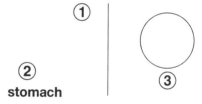

① ② **stomach** ③

1. Draw a _____ line.

2. Write the word _____ to the _____ of the line.

3. Draw a _____ to the _____ of the line.

Graphic aids, adjectives, following directions
Directions: If necessary, read the directions for each part. When students have completed the page, present each item and the answer. Correct any errors.

Part 4

For each numbered word, write the letter of the word's definition.

1. abdominal muscle _____   a. (n.) the body system of bones

2. biceps _____   b. (a.) that something is helpful

3. construct _____   c. (v.) choose

4. constructive _____   d. (n.) the muscle that goes from the ribs to the pelvis

5. muscular system _____   e. (n.) the body system of muscles

6. protection _____   f. (n.) the muscle that covers the front of the humerus

7. quadriceps _____   g. (n.) the bone that covers the brain

8. select _____   h. (v.) build

9. skeletal system _____   i. (n.) the muscle that covers the front of the femur

10. skull _____   j. (n.) something that protects

Part 5

Write a word that comes from **predict** in each blank. Fill in the correct circle next to **verb, noun,** or **adjective.**

1. The doctor is _____ that she will make a complete recovery.
   ○ verb   ○ noun   ○ adjective

2. Jake hid in a very _____ spot during the game of hide-and-seek.
   ○ verb   ○ noun   ○ adjective

3. Some people make a living making weather _____.
   ○ verb   ○ noun   ○ adjective

4. I've never read such a _____ story before.
   ○ verb   ○ noun   ○ adjective

5. I _____ that the show would sell out.
   ○ verb   ○ noun   ○ adjective

Definitions, inflectional suffixes, conventions of grammar
Directions: If necessary, read the directions for each part. When students have completed the page, present each item and the answer. Correct any errors.

LESSON 34

Part 1

Complete the instructions.

①
femur
③   △ ②

1. Draw a _____ line down to the right.

2. Draw a _____ above the right end of the line.

3. Write the word _____ below the _____ end of the line.

Part 2

Read the story and answer the questions.

> Terry and Wayne began building a new boat to sail on the pond. They searched around and found some lumber in a garbage pile. Terry said, "I want to make this boat even bigger than the last one."
> Wayne shook his head at his brother and said, "Terry, we don't have enough wood to make this boat as big as the one that sank. Either we'll have to wait to get more wood, or we'll have to make this boat smaller than the one that sank."

1. What does Terry want to do?

   _____

   _____

2. Why can't they make a boat that's bigger than the one that sank?

   _____

   _____

3. If they don't get more lumber, the boat they build will have to be _____

   _____

4. What do the boys need to build a bigger boat?

   _____

   _____

Following directions, making inferences
Directions: If necessary, read the directions for each part. When students have completed the page, present each item and the answer. Correct any errors.

Part 3

Write **biceps, abdominal muscle,** or **quadriceps** in each blank.

1. _____

2. _____

3. _____

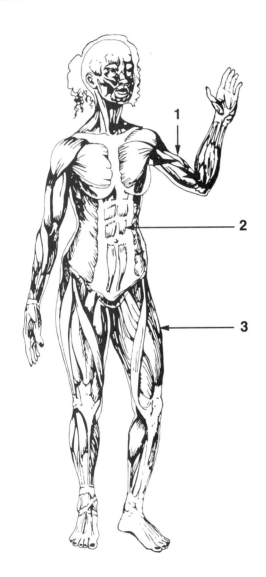

☆ Part 4

Read each sentence. Underline each **adjective**. Circle the person, place, or thing the adjective describes.

1. He liked the brown jacket.

2. I wanted raisin bread for breakfast.

3. Sherry ate three bananas today.

4. The white snow looked pretty.

5. I wished for a baby brother on my birthday.

6. The old lighthouse was close to the ocean.

7. My favorite aunt was coming for a visit.

8. Three weeks have passed since we had rain.

Graphic aids, adjectives
Directions: If necessary, read the directions for each part. When students have completed the page, present each item and the answer. Correct any errors.

Part 1

Write the number of the fact that explains why each thing happened.

1. Cows give milk.
2. Cows eat grass.

_____ a. The man who owned the cow never cut his grass.

_____ b. The man made butter at home.

_____ c. The cow ate green things.

_____ d. The man did not buy milk at the store.

Part 2

Write a word that comes from **select** or **predict** in each blank. Fill in the correct circle next to **verb, noun,** or **adjective.**

1. My video store has a wide

   _____ of movies to rent.
   ○ verb   ○ noun   ○ adjective

2. I don't like movies with _____ endings.
   ○ verb   ○ noun   ○ adjective

3. I can _____ any type of movie I want to see at my video store.
   ○ verb   ○ noun   ○ adjective

Part 3

Write **abdominal muscle, quadriceps,** or **biceps** in each blank.

1. _____

2. _____

3. _____

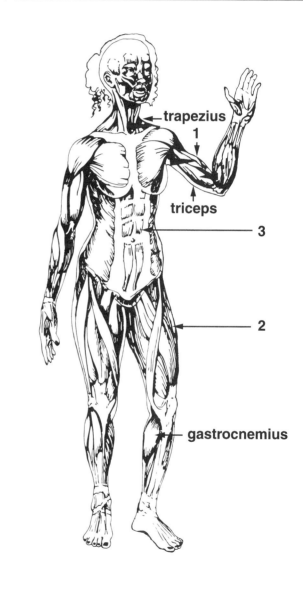

trapezius
1
triceps
3
2
gastrocnemius

Drawing conclusions based on evidence, inflectional suffixes/conventions of grammar, graphic aids
Directions: If necessary, read the directions for each part. When students have completed the page, present each item and the answer. Correct any errors.

☆ Part 4

> • An **adverb** is a word that describes a verb. It tells *how, when,* or *where.* Many adverbs end in **–ly.**
> Examples:
> The horse walked **slowly. How?**
> The horse walked **today. When?**
> The horse walked **here. Where?**

Underline each adverb. Then write **how, when,** or **where** on the lines provided.

1. Tom eats dinner late. _____

2. Amy ran quickly. _____

3. The cat sat there. _____

Complete each sentence with an adverb from the box below. Choose an adverb that answers the question in ( ).

> slowly   early   near

4. I live _____ the school. (Where?)

5. Grandma walked up the stairs _____. (How?)

6. Dad left for work _____. (When?)

Part 5

Complete the analogy.

Prediction is to noun

1. as **protect** is to _____.

2. as **selective** is to _____.

3. as **construction** is to _____.

Part 6

Underline the common part. Then combine the sentences with **and.**

1. The woman was mad.
Her husband was mad.

_____

_____

2. Monkeys were climbing in trees.
Monkeys were searching for nuts.

_____

_____

3. Clem was reading in the library.
Stan was reading in the library.

_____

_____

Adverbs, analogies, conjunctions
Directions: If necessary, read the directions for each part. When students have completed the page, present each item and the answer. Correct any errors.

Part 1

Underline each contradiction.

1. All dogs have four legs.

   a. All dogs have three legs.

   b. No dogs have four legs.

   c. Only some dogs have four legs.

   d. Every dog has four legs.

2. Jill is bigger than Carol.

   a. Jill is not bigger than Carol.

   b. Carol is smaller than Jill.

   c. Jill is smaller than Carol.

   d. Carol is not as big as Jill.

Part 2

Complete the instructions.

①

②

   _____

③

1. Draw a _____ pointing

   _____.

2. Draw a _____ pointing

   _____, under the other triangle.

3. Draw a _____ line underneath

   the _____ pointing _____.

☆ Part 3

Underline the **adverb** in each sentence. What question does the adverb answer? Write the answer on the line.

1. I walked quickly down the street.

   _____

2. She will return soon.

   _____

3. David lives across the street.

   _____

4. I will eat lunch early today.

   _____

5. The clouds are above our heads.

   _____

6. The lions roared loudly.

   _____

7. The children walked slowly into the assembly.

   _____

8. The sun shines brightly.

   _____

Contradictions, following directions, adverbs
Directions: If necessary, read the directions for each part. When students have completed the page, present each item and the answer. Correct any errors.

Part 4

Write **trapezius, triceps,** or **gastrocnemius** in each blank.

1. _____

2. _____

3. _____

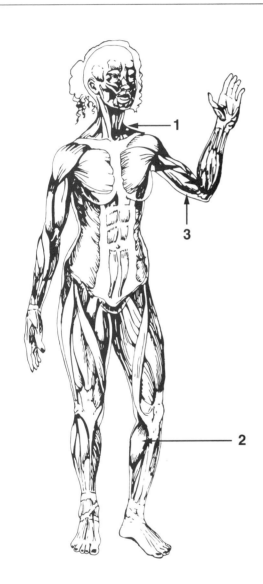

Part 5

Read the story and answer the questions. Circle the **W** if the question is answered by words in the story, and underline those words. Circle the **D** if the question is answered by a deduction.

> Kyle did not know which park to play at. He said to himself, " My sister is swimming at the Aqua Park, but my brother is playing kickball at the Athletic Field. I like both of those activities, but I think I'll go to the Aqua Park and swim, because that place will stay cooler when it gets hot this afternoon." So Kyle went to the Aqua Park.

1. Where was Kyle's brother playing kickball?

   _____ **W D**

2. Which activity did Kyle prefer?

   _____ **W D**

3. Why did Kyle choose the Aqua Park over the Athletic Field?

   _____ **W D**

4. Did Kyle like it better when it was hotter or cooler?

   _____ **W D**

Graphic aids, deductions
Directions: If necessary, read the directions for each part. When students have completed the page, present each item and the answer. Correct any errors.

☆ Part 1

The words in the box below are **adverbs.** Write each word under a heading to show if the word tells **how, when,** or **where.**

late	soon	brightly	early
loudly	yesterday	near	there
fast	here	away	slowly

How?   **When?**   **Where?**

_____   _____   _____

_____   _____   _____

_____   _____   _____

_____   _____   _____

Part 2

Complete the instructions.

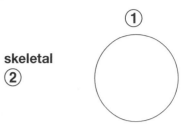

①

skeletal
②

biceps
③

1. Draw a _____.

2. Write the word _____ to the

   left of the _____.

3. Write the word **biceps** _____ the

   _____.

Part 3

Underline each contradiction.

The small intestine is in the digestive system.

a. The small intestine is a bone.

b. The small intestine protects body parts.

c. The small intestine is in the skeletal system.

d. The small intestine is in the system of muscles.

Adverbs, following directions, contradictions
Directions: If necessary, read the directions for each part. When students have completed the page, present each item and the answer. Correct any errors.

Part 4

Write **trapezius, quadriceps, gastrocnemius, biceps, abdominal muscle,** or **triceps** in each blank.

1. _____

2. _____

3. _____

4. _____

5. _____

6. _____

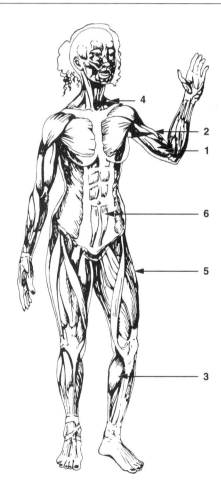

Part 5

Underline the common part. Then combine the sentences with **and.**

1. Joey was playing basketball.
   Tom was playing basketball.

   _____

   _____

2. Andre ran on the track.
   Andre listened to his radio.

   _____

   _____

3. The girls followed the creek.
   The girls found a field.

   _____

   _____

4. The teacher gave Will a detention.
   The teacher gave Will extra homework.

   _____

   _____

5. My brother was falling asleep.
   Dad was falling asleep.

   _____

   _____

Graphic aids, conjunctions
Directions: If necessary, read the directions for each part. When students have completed the page, present each item and the answer. Correct any errors.

Part 1

For each numbered word, write the letter of the word's definition.

1. prediction   _____   a. (n.) the muscle that covers the back of the humerus

2. triceps   _____   b. (n.) the muscle that covers the back of the neck

3. gastrocnemius   _____   c. (v.) build

4. construct   _____   d. (n.) something that is selected

5. selection   _____   e. (n.) the bones that cover the organs in the chest

6. trapezius   _____   f. (n.) a statement that predicts ·

7. spine   _____   g. (n.) the backbone

8. ribs   _____   h. (n.) the muscle that covers the back of the lower leg

Part 2

Underline each contradiction.

> **The triceps is a muscle.**

a. The triceps is in the muscular system.

b. The triceps is not in the skeletal system.

c. The triceps is a bone.

d. The triceps is part of the digestive system.

Definitions, contradictions
Directions: If necessary, read the directions for each part. When students have completed the page, present each item and the answer. Correct any errors.

Part 3

Complete the instructions.

② **obtained**

① ◯

examination ③

1. Draw a _____ .

2. Write the word **obtained** _____ the

_____ .

3. Write the word **examination**

_____ the _____ .

☆ Part 4

> Use a **comma (,)** after the words **yes** and **no** if they begin a sentence.
> **Example:** Yes, you may go now.
>
> Use a **comma** to separate three or more items listed together in a sentence.
> **Example:** I had juice, cereal, toast, and eggs for breakfast.

Read the sentences below. Add commas where they are needed.

1. No the band was not in the parade.

2. Horses cows pigs and goats live in the country.

3. Yes I was sick yesterday.

Part 5

Write a word that comes from **reside** in each blank. Fill in the correct circle next to **verb, noun,** or **adjective.**

1. They don't allow warehouses in

   _____ areas.
   ◯ verb   ◯ noun   ◯ adjective

2. Some people do not have permanent

   _____ .
   ◯ verb   ◯ noun   ◯ adjective

3. Many ducks _____ near water.
   ◯ verb   ◯ noun   ◯ adjective

4. An apartment is usually a cheaper

   _____ than a house.
   ◯ verb   ◯ noun   ◯ adjective

5. Firefighters actually _____ at the firehouse.
   ◯ verb   ◯ noun   ◯ adjective

Following directions, commas, inflectional suffixes/conventions of grammar
Directions: If necessary, read the directions for each part. When students have completed the page, present each item and the answer. Correct any errors.

Part 1

Write **abdominal muscle, triceps, biceps, trapezius, gastrocnemius,** or **quadriceps** for each blank.

1. _____

2. _____

3. _____

4. _____

5. _____

6. _____

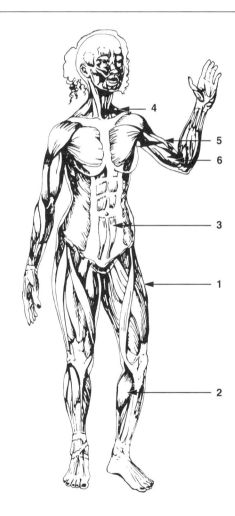

☆ Part 2

Read each sentence. Then place commas where they are needed in each sentence.

1. I sleep with a sheet a blanket and a bedspread to keep warm.

2. John's favorite foods are pizza peaches and corn.

3. Larry has lived in Ohio Kentucky and New Jersey.

4. Remember to pack the chairs cooler beach towels lotion and toys for the beach.

5. Terry's favorite subjects are math science and art.

6. Sandy has a dog a cat a rabbit and a hamster as pets.

7. Please make your bed brush your teeth walk the dog and put out the trash.

8. Let's go to the beach the museum and the zoo on our trip.

Graphic aids, commas
Directions: If necessary, read the directions for each part. When students have completed the page, present each item and the answer. Correct any errors.

Part 3

Underline the common part. Then combine the sentences with **and.**

1. Kate was protecting the candy.
   Ann was protecting the candy.

   _____

   _____

2. Maury likes oranges.
   Cynthia likes oranges.

   _____

   _____

3. Steve speaks English.
   Steve speaks Spanish.

   _____

   _____

4. Table tennis was fun to play.
   Pool was fun to play.

   _____

   _____

5. Poodles are smart.
   Poodles are peppy.

   _____

   _____

Part 4

Cross out the words that are in the rule and the conclusion. Then write the middle part.

1. Every noun names a person, place, or thing.

   _____

   _____

   So, **Lawrence** names a person, place, or thing.

2. Some dogs have straight hair.

   _____

   _____

   So, maybe a terrier has straight hair.

3. The woman found some bones.

   _____

   _____

   So, maybe the woman found a humerus.

Conjunctions, writing deductions
Directions: If necessary, read the directions for each part. When students have completed the page, present each item and the answer. Correct any errors.

Part 1

Make each contradiction true.

Steve is shorter than Jim.

1. Steve is taller than Jim.

2. Steve is not shorter than Jim.

3. Jim is shorter than Steve.

4. Jim is not shorter than Steve.

Part 2

Complete the instructions.

①   ②

③ **triceps**

1. Draw a _____ line.

2. Draw a vertical line _____ from

the _____ end of the horizontal line.

3. Write the word _____ to the left

of the _____ line.

☆ Part 3

Look at each pair of sentences. Underline the sentence in which the **commas** are correctly placed.

1. Please put away your books, pencils, and paper.

Please put away your books pencils, and paper.

2. Bill, Jane Tracy and Brad all ride the same bus.

Bill, Jane, Tracy, and Brad all ride the same bus.

3. I like to ride bikes, play video games and skateboard.

I like to ride bikes, play video games, and skateboard.

4. My favorite fruits are oranges, peaches, grapes, and watermelon.

My favorite fruits are oranges, peaches, grapes and watermelon.

5. Monday, and Wednesday I work out.

Monday and Wednesday I work out.

Contractions, following directions, commas
Directions: If necessary, read the directions for each part. When students have completed the page, present each item and the answer. Correct any errors.

Part 4

Write the conclusion of each deduction.

1. Everything you drink goes down your
esophagus.
Water is something you drink.

_____

_____

2. Some bones are joined to two other bones.
The tibia is a bone.

_____

_____

3. Jack has some dogs.
A Scottish terrier is a dog.

_____

_____

Part 5

Underline the common part. Then combine the
sentences with **and.**

1. Katie is reading a book.

   Sam is reading a book.

   _____

   _____

2. Six ducks were flying.

   A robin was flying.

   _____

   _____

3. This dog is friendly.

   That cat is friendly.

   _____

   _____

4. Sally has a headache.

   Sally has a toothache.

   _____

   _____

Deductions, conjunctions/writing
Directions: If necessary, read the directions for each part. When students have completed the page, present each item
and the answer. Correct any errors.

Part 1

Make each contradiction true.

> The biceps is in the muscular system.

1. The biceps is a bone.

2. The biceps is in the system of bones.

3. The biceps is in the digestive system.

4. A two-headed muscle is in the skeletal system.

Part 2

Cross out the words that are in the rule and the conclusion. Then write the middle part.

1. Most women have hair on their head.

_____

So, maybe Carol has hair on her head.

2. A muscle does not move the bone it covers.

_____

So, a triceps does not move the bone it covers.

3. Some nouns come from verbs.

_____

So, maybe **house** comes from a verb.

Part 3

Fill in each blank.

1. _____

2. _____

3. _____

4. _____

5. _____

6. _____

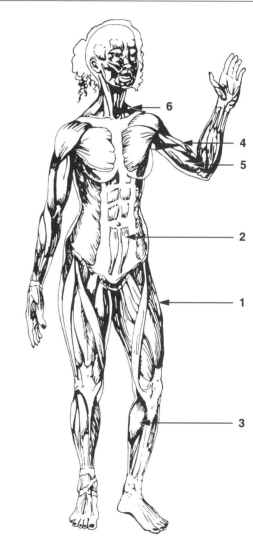

Contradictions, writing deductions, graphic aids

Directions: If necessary, read the directions for each part. When students have completed the page, present each item and the answer. Correct any errors

☆ Part 4

> Use a **capital letter** to begin most **abbreviations**.
> Use a **period** at the end of an **abbreviation**.
> Doctor Boyle **Dr.** Boyle
> Mister Carver **Mr.** Carver

Write the names. Use capital letters and periods where they are needed.

mrs crotty _____

dr thompson _____

mr lyons _____

mrs brown _____

mr lewis _____

mrs berry _____

dr timko _____

mr wilt _____

dr zimmerman _____

ms alcorn _____

Part 5

Fill in each blank with the word that has the same meaning as the word or words under the blank.

> | constructed | protect |
> |---|---|
> | reside | predict |

1. Firefighters _____
   (say it will happen)
   that smoke alarms will save lives.

2. Many bats _____ in caves.
   (live)

3. Brushing your teeth will _____
   them from decay.   (guard)

4. The stairs are _____ of wood.
   (built)

Abbreviations, vocabulary
Directions: If necessary, read the directions for each part. When students have completed the page, present each item and the answer. Correct any errors.

74   © 2001 SRA/McGraw-Hill. Permission is granted to reproduce for classroom use.

Part 1

Follow the directions.

1. Draw a line that slants down to the left.

2. Write the word **liver** at the top end of the line.

3. Write the word **mouth** at the bottom end of the line.

Part 2

Underline the common part. Then combine the sentences with **and.**

1. Joey likes to predict the weather.

   Tamara likes to predict the weather.

   _____

   _____

2. That dog has floppy ears.

   That dog has a long tail.

   _____

   _____

3. Tony has a green shirt.

   Tony has blue pants.

   _____

   _____

☆ Part 3

An initial is the first letter of a name. Capitalize an initial and put a period after it.
Example: **M. C.** Wells for **Mary Coe Wells**

Write the names. Use capital letters and periods where they are needed.

1. a c kenny   _____

2. mrs m l lewis   _____

3. mr r d willams _____

4. a a milne   _____

5. mrs p overman _____

6. e b white   _____

7. ms bacall   _____

8. r c ward   _____

Following directions, conjunctions/writing sentences, abbreviations
Directions: If necessary, read the directions for each part. When students have completed the page, present each item and the answer. Correct any errors.

Part 4

Read the story and answer the questions. Circle the **W** if the question is answered by words in the story, and underline those words. Circle the **D** if the question is answered by a deduction.

> After looking around for a month, Terry and Wayne had obtained enough wood to make a bigger boat than the one that sank. They worked for a week constructing the new boat. When it was finished, Terry wanted to launch it into the pond immediately. "Wait a second," Wayne said. "It's bad luck to launch a boat before naming it. We need a good name for it."
>
> Terry thought for a moment. "I know, why not *The Twayne?*" Wayne agreed and smiled.

1. Why did the boat need a name before Terry and Wayne launched it into the pond?

   _____

   _____

   _____ **W D**

2. How did Terry come up with the name "The Twayne" for the boat?

   _____

   _____

   _____ **W D**

Part 5

Make each contradiction true.

> **All cats have a spine.**

1. That kitten has a spine.

2. Her cat has no backbone.

3. Only some cats have a spine.

4. A few cats have a backbone.

Deductions/writing, contradictions
Directions: If necessary, read the directions for each part. When students have completed the page, present each item and the answer. Correct any errors.

Part 1

For each numbered word, write the letter of the word's definition.

1. residence	_____	a. (v.) look at
2. predictable	_____	b. (v.) live somewhere
3. humerus	_____	c. (a.) that a place has many residences
4. examine	_____	d. (n.) the hip bone
5. residential	_____	e. (n.) the upper arm bone
6. pelvis	_____	f. (n.) a place where someone resides
7. reside	_____	g. (v.) say that something will happen
8. femur	_____	h. (a.) that something protects
9. protective	_____	i. (n.) the upper leg bone
10. predict	_____	j. (a.) that something is easy to predict

Part 2

Write the number of the fact that explains why each thing happened.

1. Keri is building up her biceps.
2. Alice broke her femur.

a. She has a cast on her leg.   _____

b. She swims every other day.   _____

c. She lifts weights.   _____

d. She was in the hospital overnight.   _____

Definitions, drawing conclusions based on evidence
Directions: If necessary, read the directions for each part. When students have completed the page, present each item and the answer. Correct any errors.

☆ Part 3

> Use a capital letter to begin an
> abbreviation for the name of a place.
> **Example:**
> Road: Rd.   Street: St.   Drive: Dr.
> Avenue: Ave.   Court: Ct.

Write the name using the correct abbreviation.
Use capital letters and periods where needed.

1. maple street

_____

2. princeton road

_____

3. boston avenue

_____

4. franklin road

_____

5. forest highlands court

_____

6. riverside drive

_____

Part 4
Make each contradiction true.

> **Tia never selected a book with a
> predictable ending.**

1. The book that Tia selected had a predictable
ending.

2. Tia never chose a book with a surprise
ending.

3. Tia never selected a book that had an ending
that could be predicted.

Abbreviations, contradictions
Directions: If necessary, read the directions for each part. When students have completed the page, present each item
and the answer. Correct any errors.

Part 1

Underline the nouns. Draw a line over the adjectives. Circle the verbs.

1. Squirrels are foraging near that stream.

2. Dust swirled in the bright sunlight.

3. The playful puppies attacked his socks.

4. The beans filled the jar.

5. My computer uses a color monitor.

Part 2

Complete the instructions.

③ skeletal

①

muscular
②

1. Draw a line that slants down to the

   _____.

2. Write the word _____

   _____ the line.

3. Write the word _____

   _____ the line.

☆ Part 3

> A **pronoun** is a part of speech. It takes the place of a noun. Some pronouns are **he, she, it, we, you, they,** and **I.**
> **Example:** Will plays with Brian. He plays with Brian.

Rewrite these sentences. Choose a pronoun from the box below to take the place of the underlined word or words.

| He | She | We | They |

1. Leslie got a gift.

   _____

   _____

2. James went to the baseball game.

   _____

   _____

3. Wendy and Chris are going shopping.

   _____

   _____

4. Suzi and I like to travel together.

   _____

   _____

Conventions of grammar, following directions, pronouns
Directions: If necessary, read the directions for each part. When students have completed the page, present each item and the answer. Correct any errors.

Part 4

Fill in the circle next to **one** or **more than one** after each sentence. Write **were** or **was** in each blank.

1. The boy _____ sad.
   ○ one   ○ more than one

2. His brother _____ sad.
   ○ one   ○ more than one

3. The boys _____ sad.
   ○ one   ○ more than one

4. Those girls and that boy _____ sad.
   ○ one   ○ more than one

Part 5

Make each contradiction true.

> **That dog always protects this yard.**

1. This yard is always protected by that dog.

2. This yard is never guarded by that dog.

3. The dog never gives this yard protection.

4. That dog sometimes protects this yard.

Part 6

Fill in each blank.

1. _____

2. _____

3. _____

4. _____

5. _____

6. _____

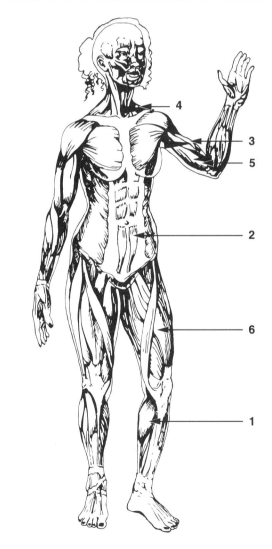

Conventions of grammar, contradictions, graphic aids
Directions: If necessary, read the directions for each part. When students have completed the page, present each item and the answer. Correct any errors.

Part 1

Fill in each blank.

1. _____
2. _____
3. _____
4. _____
5. _____
6. _____

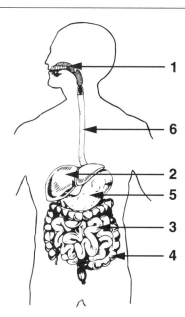

1 — →

6 — →

2 —

5 —

3 —

4 —

Part 2

Make each contradiction true.

> **Only an adjective describes a person, place, or thing.**

1. Some verbs describe a place.

2. **Dog** is an adjective.

3. **Beautiful** can describe a person, place, or thing.

4. **Chicago** names a place.

Part 3

Write the number of the fact that explains why each thing happened.

1. Sam is protective of his CDs.
2. Scott makes predictions about movie endings.

a. He uses cleaner on his collection.   ___

b. He says how the movie will end.   ___

c. He keeps his CDs in their cases.   ___

d. He says that things will happen.   ___

Graphic aids, contradictions, drawing conclusions based on evidence
Directions: If necessary, read the directions for each part. When students have completed the page, present each item and the answer. Correct any errors.

☆ Part 4

Circle the pronouns in each sentence.

1. We visited the Statue of Liberty.

2. The ranger gave us a tour.

3. He showed us the movie.

4. We went to Ellis Island, too.

5. I liked it the best!

6. Maybe we can go back next year.

7. It took a long time to get home.

8. We all slept well that night.

Part 5

Write what each analogy tells.

- What part of speech each word is
- What verb each word comes from
- What each word means
- What ending each word has

1. **Construction** is to **noun** as **protection** is to **noun.**

   _____

   _____

2. **Residence** is to **ence** as **protection** is to **ion.**

   _____

   _____

3. **Construction** is to **construct** as **residence** is to **reside.**

   _____

   _____

Pronouns, analogies

Directions: If necessary, read the directions for each part. When students have completed the page, present each item and the answer. Correct any errors.

☆ Part 1

Read each sentence. Write the pronoun that best fits the meaning.

1. The dog played with the bone and then

   buried _____.

2. Jason said, "Please give the paper to

   _____."

3. The boy said _____ heard a loud noise.

4. Gretchen lost _____ glove.

5. The family ate and discussed _____ plans for the day.

6. Mike asked if we could meet _____.

7. Will Gary and Lyn fly when _____ go to Florida?

8. Sally said _____ cold was getting better.

Part 2

Underline the common part. Then combine the sentences with **and.**

1. Joe ate his cereal.
   Joe ate his toast.

   _____

   _____

2. Amy selected a book
   Amy selected a CD.

   _____

   _____

3. Vince shot several jump shots.
   Vince shot several free throws.

   _____

   _____

4. Nigel ran with his dog.
   Nigel ran with Liane.

   _____

   _____

5. Homer is very funny.
   Homer is very wise.

   _____

   _____

Pronouns, conjunctions/writing sentences
Directions: If necessary, read the directions for each part. When students have completed the page, present each item and the answer. Correct any errors.

Part 3

Write what each analogy tells.

- What body system each thing is in
- How many parts
- What bone each thing covers

1. **Quadriceps** is to **femur** as **triceps** is to **humerus.**

_____

_____

2. **Quadriceps** is to the **muscular system** as **biceps** is to the **muscular system.**

_____

_____

3. **Quadriceps** is to **four** as **biceps** is to **two.**

_____

_____

Part 4

Cross out the words that are in the rule and the conclusion. Then write the middle part.

1. Lonnie has some cats.

_____

So, maybe Lonnie has a Siamese.

2. Some words are not nouns.

_____

So, maybe **silly** is not a noun.

3. Every muscle does a job.

_____

So, the triceps does a job.

Part 5

Follow the directions.

1. Draw a horizontal line.

2. Draw a vertical line down from the center of the horizontal line.

3. Write the word skeletal at the bottom of the vertical line.

Analogies/writing analogies, following directions
Directions: If necessary, read the directions for each part. When students have completed the page, present each item and the answer. Correct any errors.

Name _____

Part 1

Write **who** or **which** after each item.

1. Four women _____
2. His dad _____
3. His hat _____
4. Our teacher _____
5. Two spoons _____
6. Her liver _____
7. A young woman _____
8. His skin _____
9. Those cows _____
10. An orange _____

Part 2

Make each statement mean the same thing as the statement in the box.

> **The trainer examined Cory's quadriceps.**

1. The trainer looked at Cory's three-headed muscle.

2. The trainer examined Cory's triceps.

3. The trainer looked at Cory's quadriceps.

☆ Part 3

> A **prefix** comes before a base word. Below are some examples of **prefixes.**
>
> **un**tied   **dis**obey   **re**draw
>
> The prefixes **un-** and **dis-** often mean "not." The prefix **re-** may mean "again."

Indicate the word that correctly completes each sentence by filling in the circle.

1. It will be _____ if we can't go to the party.
   ○ fair   ○ unfair   ○ unright

2. If you _____ the television, it won't work.
   ○ reconnect   ○ disconnect   ○ connect

3. Don't be afraid to _____ if you have a good reason.
   ○ disagree   ○ reagree   ○ unagree

4. Toby was _____ of the formula.
   ○ dissure   ○ resure   ○ unsure

5. Dad will _____ the shed.
   ○ rebuild   ○ unbuild   ○ disbuild

Conventions of grammar, making inferences, prefixes
Directions: If necessary, read the directions for each part. When students have completed the page, present each item and the answer. Correct any errors

Part 4

Fill in each blank.

1. _____

2. _____

3. _____

4. _____

5. _____

6. _____

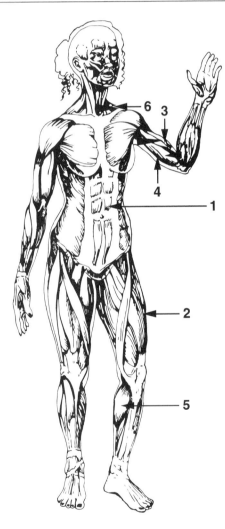

Part 5

Use the rule to answer the questions.

> **The more milk you drink,
> the more vitamins you get.**

1. Aaron drinks four glasses of milk a week.
   Ed drinks six glasses of milk a week.
   a. Who gets more vitamins from milk?

   _____

   b. How do you know?

   _____

   _____

2. Sandy drinks two gallons of milk a week.
   Cindy drinks three gallons of milk a week.
   a. Who gets more vitamins from milk?

   _____

   b. How do you know?

   _____

   _____

Graphic aids, making inferences
Directions: If necessary, read the directions for each part. When students have completed the page, present each item and the answer. Correct any errors.

Name _____

Part 1

For each numbered word, write the letter of the word's definition.

1. obtain _____   a. (v.) build

2. mouth _____   b. (a.) that a place has many residences

3. criticize _____   c. (n.) the organ that mixes food with chemicals

4. reside _____   d. (n.) the system that changes food into fuel for the body

5. construct _____   e. (v.) get

6. residence _____   f. (v.) find fault with

7. stomach _____   g. (n.) the part that takes in solid and liquid food

8. digestive system _____   h. (v.) live somewhere

9. residential _____   i. (n.) a place where someone resides

10. esophagus _____   j. (n.) the tube that goes from the mouth to the stomach

Part 2

Make each statement mean the same thing as the statement in the box.

> **The protective father constructed a stronger crib.**

1. The father who was protective built a crib that would last longer.

2. The father who constructed a stronger crib was protective.

3. The protective father built a crib that was weaker.

4. The careless father built a stronger crib.

Definitions, contradictions
Directions: If necessary, read the directions for each part. When students have completed the page, present each item and the answer. Correct any errors.

Part 3

Write the number of the fact that explains why each thing happened.

1. Tina's triceps pulled.

2. Lisa's lower leg bone moved.

a. The muscle that pulled was in her upper arm. ____

b. She pulled with a muscle that covered her femur. ____

c. The muscle that pulled was in her leg. ____

Part 4

Write **who** or **which** after each item.

1. His grandfather _____

2. Her table _____

3. My stomach _____

4. Her little brother _____

5. That woman _____

6. His humerus _____

7. Three bushes _____

8. A watermelon _____

☆ Part 5

> The prefixes **un-** and **dis-** often mean "not." The prefix **re-** often means "again."

Underline each word with a prefix. On the line write what the word means.

1. His shoelace is untied.

_____

2. My dog disobeys me sometimes.

_____

3. Thomas will rebuild his engine.

_____

4. This rock is unlike any I have ever seen.

_____

5. Brian said that he disagrees with you.

_____

6. I wish you would recopy your thank you letter.

_____

Drawing conclusions based on evidence, conventions of grammar, definitions/prefixes
Directions: If necessary, read the directions for each part. When students have completed the page, present each item and the answer. Correct any errors.

☆ Part 1

> The prefixes **un-** and **dis-** often mean "not." The prefix **re-** often means "again."

Complete each sentence by adding **un-, dis-,** or **re-** to the word in parentheses ( ).

1. Should I _____ your dinner?
   (heat)

2. The magician made the woman

   _____. (appear)

3. The man looked _____ about the
   accident.   (concerned)

4. I want to _____ that wrapping
   paper.   (use)

5. You have time to _____ your
   suitcase.   (pack)

6. Will tried to _____ where the
   water was coming in. (cover)

Part 2

Fill in each blank.

1. _____

2. _____

3. _____

4. _____

5. _____

6. _____

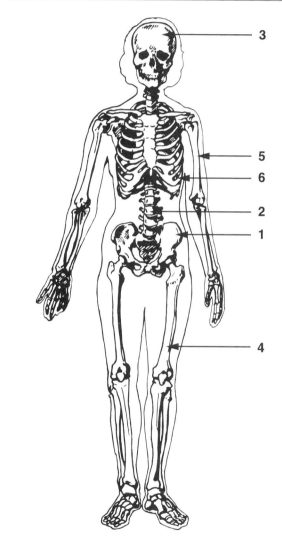

Prefixes, graphic aids
Directions: If necessary, read the directions for each part. When students have completed the page, present each item and the answer. Correct any errors.

Part 3

Write the number of the fact that explains why each thing happened.

1. Joe described a thing.
2. Frank told the action that things do.

a. He said a word like **learn.**   ___

b. He said a verb.   ___

c. He said an adjective.   ___

d. He said a word like **simple.**   ___

Part 4

Complete the instructions.

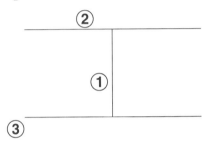

1. Draw a _____ line.

2. Draw a _____ line at the

   _____ of the vertical line.

3. Draw a _____ line at the

   _____ of the vertical line.

Part 5

Underline the common part. Then combine the sentences with **who** or **which.**

1. Noel is fascinated by her little sister.
   Her little sister is only six months old.

   _____

   _____

   _____

2. Tim's father is calling for Tim.
   Tim is in the closet.

   _____

   _____

3. He hurt his triceps.
   His triceps covers his humerus.

   _____

   _____

4. The little girl obtained those marbles.
   Those marbles are blue.

   _____

   _____

Drawing conclusions based on evidence, following directions, conventions of grammar/writing sentences
Directions: If necessary, read the directions for each part. When students have completed the page, present each item and the answer. Correct any errors.

Part 1

Write **R** for each fact that is **relevant** to what happened. Write **I** for each fact that is **irrelevant** to what happened.

The cat scratched the plumber.

1. The cat had black stripes. ___

2. The plumber is thirty years old. ___

3. The plumber yelled at the cat before the cat scratched him. ___

4. The cat did not like people. ___

Part 2

Write the conclusion of each deduction.

1. Most people have hair.
   Dennis is a person.

   _____

   _____

2. Muscles do not move the bones they cover.
   A quadriceps is a muscle.

   _____

   _____

3. Fish breathe under water.
   A carp is a fish.

   _____

   _____

Part 3

Fill in each blank with the word that has the same meaning as the word or words under the blank.

1. A groundhog _____ in our backyard.   (lives)

2. Selma was able to _____ food for her dog from the store. (get)

3. _____ can be helpful.
   (statements that criticize)

4. Terry _____ Duane for his team.
                (chose)

Part 4

Underline the nouns. Draw a line over the adjectives. Circle the verbs.

1. The man hurt his left quadriceps during the race.

2. The humerus is in the upper arm.

3. The digestive system includes many organs.

4. That woman selects colorful uniforms for the teams in our league.

Main idea/relevant and irrelevant details, deductions, vocabulary, conventions of grammar
Directions: If necessary, read the directions for each part. When students have completed the page, present each item and the answer. Correct any errors.

☆ Part 5

> A **suffix** is added at the end of a word.
>
> thank**ful**   enjoy**ment**   quick**ly**
>
> The suffix **–ful** often means "full of."
> The suffix **–less** often means "without."
> The suffix **–er** often means "one who does."
> The suffix **–ment** often means "the act of."

Underline each word that has a suffix.
Fill in the circle next to the phrase that describes what the word means.

1. The builder bought nails and screws to construct a house.
   ○ one who buys   ○ one who builds

2. Be careful when you play with the puppy.
   ○ full of care   ○ full of play

3. It looked hopeless for my baseball team when we were down nine runs.
   ○ without runs   ○ without hope

4. The paintings in the museum were beautiful.
   ○ full of beauty   ○ full of paint

Part 6

Underline the common part. Then combine the sentences with **who** or **which.**

1. Doing pull-ups hardens your biceps.
   Your biceps are part of your upper arms.

   _____

   _____

   _____

2. The girl drinks milk.
   Milk is good for her.

   _____

   _____

3. Everyone is born with soft bones.
   Soft bones harden as we grow.

   _____

   _____

4. Everyone has hair.
   Hair helps trap body heat.

   _____

   _____

Suffixes, conventions of grammar/writing sentences
Directions: If necessary, read the directions for each part. When students have completed the page, present each item and the answer. Correct any errors.

Part 1

Cross out the words that are in the rule and the conclusion. Write the middle part.

1. Pat examined some bones.

_____

So, maybe Pat examined a rib.

2. Nouns do not tell how many.

_____

So, **construction** does not tell how many.

3. Some plants can grow without direct sunlight.

_____

So, maybe moss can grow without direct sunlight.

Part 2

Write **R** for each fact that is **relevant** to what happened. Write **I** for each fact that is **irrelevant** to what happened.

The man honked his horn.

1. He was wearing a baseball cap.   ___

2. He was angry with the driver in front of him.   ___

3. He had a blue truck.   ___

4. He liked to be loud.   ___

Part 3

Fill in each blank.

1. _____

2. _____

3. _____

4. _____

5. _____

6. _____

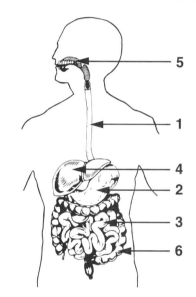

Writing deductions, main idea/relevant and irrelevant details, graphic aids
Directions: If necessary, read the directions for each part. When students have completed the page, present each item and the answer. Correct any errors.

Part 4

Underline the common part. Then combine the sentences with **who** or **which.**

1. Kerry selected some flowers for Carly.
Carly is sick.

_____

_____

2. Two men constructed that dog house.
That dog house is hidden by trees.

_____

_____

3. Six tall boys play ball on that court.
That court has regulation basketball hoops.

_____

_____

4. Their Doberman protects their house.
Their house contains many valuables.

_____

_____

_____

☆ Part 5

Using the box below, add a suffix to each word. Tell what the new word means.

-ful   -er   -ment

1. fear   Word: _____

          Meaning: _____

2. work   Word: _____

          Meaning: _____

3. cheer   Word: _____

          Meaning: _____

4. enjoy   Word: _____

          Meaning: _____

5. help   Word: _____

          Meaning: _____

6. hope   Word: _____

          Meaning: _____

Conventions of grammar/writing sentences, suffixes
Directions: If necessary, read the directions for each part. When students have completed the page, present each item and the answer. Correct any errors.

Part 1

Write what each analogy tells.

- What ending each word has
- What part of speech each word is
- What each word means
- What verb each word comes from

1. Constructive is to **adjective** as **prediction** is to **noun.**

_____

_____

2. Constructive is to **construct** as **prediction** is to **predict.**

_____

_____

3. Constructive is to **ive** as **prediction** is to **ion.**

_____

_____

☆ Part 2

Using the words in the box complete the sentences below.

tireless	careful	successful
spoonful	quickly	teacher

1. Please be _____ when you open the door.

2. My _____ says that I am a good writer.

3. Try a _____ of custard.

4. Being _____ takes a lot of hard work and dedication.

5. I ran home _____ before the rain started.

6. She is _____ when it comes to practicing for her recital.

Analogies, suffixes

Directions: If necessary, read the directions for each part. When students have completed the page, present each item and the answer. Correct any errors.

Part 3

Make each contradiction true.

> **It is hard to predict what shoppers will select.**

1. It is not easy to say what selections shoppers will make.

2. It is easy to make predictions about what shoppers will choose.

3. It is hard to say what shoppers will choose.

4. Saying what shoppers will choose is easy.

Part 4

The predictable ending to the book left Anton

unsatisfied.

1. Underline the words that tell what left Anton unsatisfied.

2. Draw a line over the words that tell what the book did.

3. Draw a box over the words that tell what kind of ending.

Part 5

Read the story and answer the questions. Circle the **W** if the question is answered by words in the story, and underline those words. Circle the **D** if the question is answered by a deduction.

> After naming their boat *The Twayne,* Terry and Wayne prepared to launch it into the pond. They laid pipes parallel to the shoreline, then rolled the boat over them to the water. One pipe rolled into the pond, but the boat made it safely into the water.
>
> Wayne took a piece of rope that was already tied to the boat and tied it to a stump on the shore so the boat wouldn't drift away. "Now we can sail whenever we want," Terry said.
>
> Wayne nodded. "We should only go out together, though," he said. "That way, we can watch out for each other."

1. Why did Terry and Wayne lay pipes parallel to the shoreline?

_____

_____ **W D**

2. Why will Terry and Wayne only take the boat out together?

_____

_____ **W D**

Contradictions, following directions, deductions
Directions: If necessary, read the directions for each part. When students have completed the page, present each item and the answer. Correct any errors.

Name _____

Part 1

For each numbered word, write the letter of the word's definition.

1. criticize _____ a. (v.) guard

2. arteries _____ b. (n.) the very small tubes that connect arteries and veins

3. heart _____ c. (n.) the tubes that carry blood back to the heart

4. capillaries _____ d. (a.) careful about selecting things

5. predictable _____ e. (n.) the body system that moves blood around the body

6. protect _____ f. (n.) a statement that criticizes

7. circulatory system _____ g. (n.) a statement that predicts

8. selective _____ h. (v.) find fault with

9. prediction _____ i. (v.) look at

10. veins _____ j. (a.) that something is easy to predict

11. criticism _____ k. (n.) the tubes that carry blood away from the heart

12. examine _____ l. (n.) the pump that moves the blood

Definitions
Directions: If necessary, read the directions for each part. When students have completed the page, present each item and the answer. Correct any errors.

☆ Part 2

> Many words have more than one meaning. Example:
> Please be *patient* while we wait for the bus.
> He was the doctor's first *patient* today.
>
> To tell which meaning is being used:
> • Look at the rest of the sentence.
> • Decide which meaning of the word makes the most sense in the sentence.

Look at the underlined word in each sentence. Fill in the circle next to the meaning of the word that fits the sentence.

1. Mom asked him to turn on the outside <u>light</u>.
   ○ something by which we see
   ○ not heavy

2. The animal was <u>light</u> enough to jump onto a thin branch.
   ○ something by which we see
   ○ not heavy

3. I heard the dog <u>bark</u> at the squirrel.
   ○ hard outside covering of a tree
   ○ the sound a dog makes

4. The <u>bark</u> of the tree was dark brown.
   ○ hard outside covering of a tree
   ○ the sound a dog makes

Part 3

Write **R** for each fact that is **relevant** to what happened. Write **I** for each fact that is **irrelevant** to what happened.

Karen ate a big dinner last night.

1. She didn't like to exercise.   _____

2. She had not eaten since breakfast.   _____

3. She sat next to her brother at the table.   _____

4. She had heard her stomach rumbling all day.   _____

Part 4

Underline the nouns. Draw a line over the adjectives. Circle the verbs.

1. Her brother criticized the short movie.

2. The pond had many birds and many mosquitoes.

3. Airplanes were flying in the clear sky.

4. The football player predicted the final score.

5. These three musicians played those CDs.

Multiple-meaning words, main idea/relevant and irrelevant details, conventions of grammar
Directions: If necessary, read the directions for each part. When students have completed the page, present each item and the answer. Correct any errors.

Part 1

Read the story and answer the questions. Circle the **W** if the question is answered by words in the story, and underline those words. Circle the **D** if the question is answered by a deduction.

> One day during the summer, Terry wanted to take the boat out on the pond. However, Wayne was at a lesson. Terry remembered that Wayne had said they should always take the boat out together. That way, they could help each other if there was a problem. Terry didn't want to wait for Wayne, though, so he pulled the rope off the stump and got in the boat. He sailed out to the middle of the pond. Without Wayne, he had a difficult time steering the boat. After twenty minutes of struggling with the boat, Terry headed for shore. He jumped out of the boat. "I think I'll go see if Wayne is home yet," he said.

1. What did Terry want to do at the beginning of the story?

   _____ **W D**

2. Why did Wayne think he and Terry should only use the boat together?

   _____
   _____ **W D**

3. What will Terry tell Wayne?

   _____ **W D**

Part 2

Cross out the words that are in the rule and the conclusion. Then write the middle part.

1. Cats do not have gills.

   _____

   _____

   So, Princess does not have gills.

2. Every one-syllable word has a vowel.

   _____

   _____

   So, **brought** has a vowel.

3. Howard has every kind of tool.

   _____

   _____

   So, Howard has a wrench.

4. All humans have a heart.

   _____

   _____

   So, Leon has a heart.

Making inferences, writing deductions
Directions: If necessary, read the directions for each part. When students have completed the page, present each item and the answer. Correct any errors.

Part 3

Write **R** for each fact that is **relevant** to what happened. Write **I** for each fact that is **irrelevant** to what happened.

There were crows in the cornfield.

1. There was a road next to the field. ____

2. There wasn't a scarecrow. ____

3. The corn was ready to be picked. ____

4. It was sunny. ____

Part 4

Make each statement mean the same thing as the statement in the box.

People praised Stuart for his car.

1. Stuart was criticized for his automobile.

2. People were unable to find fault with Stuart's car.

3. Stuart was laughed at for his car.

4. People complimented Stuart on his automobile.

☆ Part 5

Read each sentence below, noting the underlined word. Then, fill in the circle next to the definition that best matches the meaning of the underlined word.

1. The slice of bread had strawberry <u>jam</u> on it.
   ○ a difficult problem
   ○ a spread made of fruit and sugar
   ○ to push or squeeze together

2. From the plane, Terry saw her aunt <u>wave</u> good-bye.
   ○ to sway
   ○ a moving ridge of water
   ○ to move the hand in signal

3. The boy lost his turn because he didn't play <u>fair.</u>
   ○ following the rules
   ○ sunny
   ○ treating everyone alike

4. Kim skinned his knee on the rough <u>bark</u> of the log.
   ○ to speak in a mean, loud manner
   ○ a sound that a dog makes
   ○ the outside covering of a tree trunk

Main idea/relevant and irrelevant details, making inferences, multiple-meaning words
Directions: If necessary, read the directions for each part. When students have completed the page, present each item and the answer. Correct any errors.

☆ Part 1

Fill in the circle next to the correct meaning for each underlined word.

1. The rain continued to <u>beat</u> against the house.
   ○ to mix
   ○ strike over and over

2. A <u>tear</u> rolled down the baby's cheek.
   ○ salty liquid from the eye
   ○ rip or pull apart

3. Suddenly, the warning bell began to <u>ring</u>.
   ○ narrow circle of metal worn on the finger
   ○ make the sound of a bell

4. The <u>racket</u> outside makes it hard to hear.
   ○ loud noise
   ○ light bat used in sports

Part 2

Write the number of the fact that explains why each thing happened.

1. A dog ran through the residence.
2. A dog ran through the park.

a. The dog scared some geese.　____

b. The dog tracked mud inside.　____

c. The dog knocked over a lamp.　____

d. The dog splashed through a pond.　____

Part 3

Write **R** for each fact that is **relevant** to what happened. Write **I** for each fact that is **irrelevant** to what happened.

Gale rode his bike to school.

1. He went to bed late.　____

2. He liked riding his bike.　____

3. He had a lot of homework.　____

4. He lived a few blocks from school.　____

5. He had a new mountain bike.　____

Multiple-meaning words, drawing conclusions based on evidence, main idea/relevant and irrelevant details
Directions: If necessary, read the directions for each part. When students have completed the page, present each item and the answer. Correct any error

Part 4

Fill in the circle next to the word that has the same meaning as the word or words under the blank.

1. The doctor is _____ him for
   (finding fault with)
   eating unhealthful food.
   ○ criticizing   ○ praising   ○ warning

2. She _____ on the west side
   (lives)
   of town.
   ○ stays   ○ resides   ○ works

3. If you have a good knowledge of the teams,

   you might be able to _____
   (say that it will happen)
   which will win.

   ○ decide   ○ guarantee   ○ predict

4. Dogs are used to _____
   (guard)
   many homes.
   ○ amuse   ○ protect   ○ chase

Vocabulary
Directions: If necessary, read the directions for each part. When students have completed the page, present each item and the answer. Correct any errors.

☆ Part 1

> Some nouns have irregular plural forms. These do not follow a pattern. Here are some examples:
> **woman   women / tooth   teeth**

Write the plural form of each of the following nouns.

1. foot _____

2. child _____

3. mouse _____

4. man _____

5. ox _____

6. goose _____

Write the singular form for each of the following plural forms.

7. children _____

8. oxen _____

9. women _____

10. teeth _____

Part 2

Underline the common part. Fill in the circle next to the word that will combine the sentences correctly. Combine the sentences with that word.

1. The dentist examined the teeth.
The teeth were rotten.
○ and   ○ which   ○ who

_____

_____

2. The CD was old.
Cindy sold the CD.
○ and   ○ which   ○ who

_____

_____

3. The players were frustrated.
The referee was frustrated.
○ and   ○ which   ○ who

_____

_____

4. Warren tore down the old birdbath.
Warren tore down the old shed.
○ and   ○ which   ○ who

_____

_____

Irregular plurals, conventions of grammar/writing sentences
Directions: If necessary, read the directions for each part. When students have completed the page, present each item and the answer. Correct any errors.

Part 3

Write the middle part of each deduction.

1. Kyle did not look at any simians.

_____

So, Kyle didn't look at any monkeys.
2. Burning things need oxygen.

_____

So, fires need oxygen.

Part 4

Complete the instructions.

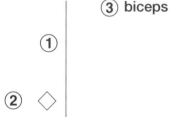

1. Draw a _____ line.

2. Draw a _____ to the

_____ of the _____ end of

the line.

3. Write the word _____ to the

_____ of the_____end of the

line.

Part 5

Make each contradiction true.

> **Action stars in movies are usually big men.**

1. Movie action stars are not that large.

2. Big men usually get the action roles in movies.

3. Small men are almost always action stars.

4. Large guys never star in action movies.

Part 6

Write the number of the fact that explains why each thing happened.

1. Bob said a noun.
2. Mitch said a verb.

a. He said a word like **constructed.**   ____

b. He named a place.   ____

c. He said a word like **construction.**   ____

Deductions, following directions, contradictions, drawing conclusions based on evidence
Directions: If necessary, read the directions for each part. When students have completed the page, present each item and the answer. Correct any errors.

☆ Part 1

A few nouns have the same singular and plural form.	
Singular	**Plural**
deer	deer
moose	moose
sheep	sheep
reindeer	reindeer

Read each sentence. Underline the correct plural form of the word in parentheses.

1. It took three (mans, men) to move the piano.

2. The (oxes, oxen) pulled the heavy wagons.

3. The boy lost two (teeth, tooths) at lunch.

4. My (feet, foots) are swollen.

5. The (mice, mouses) ran under the bed.

6. Did the (childs, children) go to bed?

7. We saw the (deers, deer) in the forest.

8. The (women, womans) were planning a vacation.

9. All the (sheeps, sheep) were in the barn.

10. Two (moose, mooses) stood by the water tower.

Part 2

Tell which fact each statement contradicts.

1. Some dogs cannot bark.
2. All dogs have four legs.

a. Every dog barks at night. ____

b. That dog ran on two legs. ____

c. All dogs bark at people they do not know. ____

d. All border collies have only three legs. ____

Part 3

Write the middle part of the deduction.

1. Most years have 365 days.

_____

So, maybe 2002 has 365 days.

2. Nouns do not tell what things do.

_____

So, **selection** does not tell what things do.

3. Some vehicles have pistons.

_____

So, maybe a jet has pistons.

Irregular plurals, contradictions, deductions
Directions: If necessary, read the directions for each part. When students have completed the page, present each item and the answer. Correct any errors.

Part 4

Complete the instructions.

② / ①
◄──────────────
③ \

1. Draw a _____ _____.

2. Draw a line that _____

   _____ _____ _____ left end

   of the _____.

3. Draw a line that _____

   _____ _____ _____ left end of

   the _____ line.

Part 5

Underline the common part. Fill in the circle next to the word that combines the sentences correctly. Combine the sentences with that word.

1. That man works at a bakery.
   His son works at a bakery.
   ○ and   ○ who   ○ which

   _____

   _____

2. The case protected the CD.
   The CD contained his favorite song.
   ○ and   ○ who   ○ which

   _____

   _____

3. Tom has red hair.
   Christina has red hair.
   ○ and   ○ who   ○ which

   _____

   _____

Writing directions, conventions of grammar/writing sentences
Directions: If necessary, read the directions for each part. When students have completed the page, present each item and the answer. Correct any errors.

Part 1

For each numbered word, write the letter of the word's definition.

1. critical _____   a. (a.) helps to explain what happened

2. construct _____   b. (a.) does not help to explain what happened

3. relevant _____   c. (n.) the organ that gives food to the blood

4. liver _____   d. (v.) build

5. reside _____   e. (n.) the organ that stores food the body cannot use

6. constructive _____   f. (v.) live somewhere

7. large intestine _____   g. (a.) that something is helpful

8. irrelevant _____   h. (n.) the organ that makes chemicals to break down food

9. muscular system _____   i. (a.) that something criticizes

10. small intestine _____   j. (n.) the body system of muscles

☆ Part 2

Read the following sentences. Write the correct plural form above each underlined word.

The womans took the childs to the zoo. There they saw mooses and sheeps. While they were eating their lunches, a girl lost two teeths. Before leaving, all of the childs put their feets in the fountain.

Definitions, irregular plurals
Directions: If necessary, read the directions for each part. When students have completed the page, present each item and the answer. Correct any errors.

Part 3

Underline the common part. Fill in the circle next to the word that combines the sentences correctly. Combine the sentences with that word.

1. Doug likes going to concerts with Tom.
Tom enjoys a good show.
○ and   ○ who   ○ which

_____

_____

2. Football is a hard game.
Football requires a lot of concentration.
○ and   ○ who   ○ which

_____

_____

3. Dogs like to run.
Dogs like to chew.
○ and   ○ who   ○ which

_____

_____

Part 4

Read the story and answer the questions. Circle the **W** if the question is answered by words in the story, and underline those words. Circle the **D** if the question is answered by a deduction.

> After Wayne got back from his music lesson, he and Terry walked to the pond. When they reached the shore, they saw that the boat had drifted into the middle of the pond. "Oh, no, I forgot to tie up the boat," Terry moaned. He looked at Wayne, who just smiled.
>
> "These things happen," Wayne said. "Now we have to figure out how to get the boat back to shore."
>
> Terry asked, "Are we going to have to swim to the boat?"
>
> Wayne nodded. "It sure looks far away," Terry said.
>
> Wayne said, "We'll wear life jackets to be safe, in case we get tired." Wayne threw his arm over his brother's shoulder and said, "Let's get ready."

1. Why did Terry think he had forgotten to tie up the boat?

_____

_____ **W D**

2. Did Wayne get mad at his brother for not

tying up the boat? _____ **W D**

3. How were the boys going to get ready at the

end of the story? _____ **W D**

Conventions of grammar/writing sentences, deductions
Directions: If necessary, read the directions for each part. When students have completed the page, present each item and the answer. Correct any errors.

☆ Part 1

Below are some words that tell the **time,** or when things happen.

today, this morning, once upon a time

Below are some words that tell the **order** in which things happen.
first, then, finally

Read the sentences. Underline every **time** or **order** word in each sentence.

1. Who went first to get ice cream?

2. Once upon a time, the trolls ruled the mountain.

3. I went to the doctor yesterday.

4. If we clean up the yard first, we can play basketball later.

5. They launched a space shuttle this morning.

6. My magazine finally came in the mail.

7. Dad had to go to New York today.

8. What was the last thing he told you before he left?

Part 2

Circle the subject.

1. The old woman went to the park.

2. Two boys and a girl sat on the curb.

3. My three sisters swim well.

4. The dog sat alone under the tree.

5. She ran through the park.

6. Ted's dad was happy it was after 3:00.

7. The soccer ball rolled into the net.

8. The car skidded off the road.

9. The clouds looked like animals.

10. The clowns are in the car.

Part 3

Write **R** for each fact that is **relevant** to what happened. Write **I** for each fact that is **irrelevant** to what happened.

Kendall's bike had a flat tire.

1. The bike had a new seat.   ___

2. There was a nail in the tire.   ___

3. She was so mad that she kicked the bike.   ___

Sequence signal words, conventions of grammar, main idea/relevant and irrelevant details
Directions: If necessary, read the directions for each part. When students have completed the page, present each item and the answer. Correct any errors.

Part 4

Write **bronchial tubes, trachea,** or **lungs** in each blank.

1. _____

2. _____

3. _____

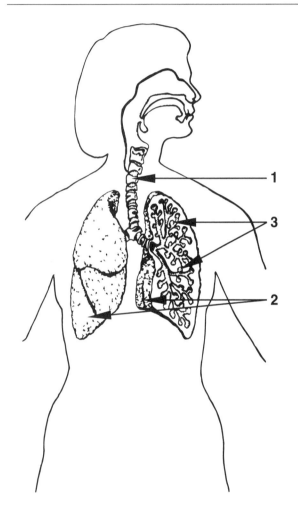

Part 5

Write a word that comes from **produce** in each blank. Then fill in the circle next to **verb, adjective,** or **noun.**

1. The Egyptians are a very

_____ people.
○ verb   ○ adjective   ○ noun

2. That company once _____ blue jeans.
○ verb   ○ adjective   ○ noun

3. Our class is _____ a display about the planets.
○ verb   ○ adjective   ○ noun

4. The report says that car

_____ went down last month.
○ verb   ○ adjective   ○ noun

Graphic aids, conventions of grammar
Directions: If necessary, read the directions for each part. When students have completed the page, present each item and the answer. Correct any errors.

Part 1

Circle the subject.

1. He has big muscles in his arms.

2. Those trees, bushes, and flowers look great.

3. This bagel is chewy and tasty.

4. People like to sing along with the band at concerts.

5. Horace and his brother like to read scary books.

6. Cordless telephones are very useful.

Part 2

Write **R** for each fact that is **relevant** to what happened. Write **I** for each fact that is **irrelevant** to what happened.

The man constructed a house.

1. He needed a place to live.   ____

2. His hair was red.   ____

3. He couldn't afford to hire someone.   ____

4. He likes to swim.   ____

☆ Part 3

Read each sentence. Underline the **time** and **order** words in each sentence. Then, write **time** if it is a time word or **order** if it is an order word.

1. This afternoon, I rode my bike.

_____

2. First, I changed my clothes.

_____

3. Then, I went to the garage

_____

4. Finally, I got on my bike.

_____

5. I rode to my friend's house, then to the school. _____

6. After I got home, it was time for dinner.

_____

7. Then, my brother and I did the dishes.

_____

8. Tomorrow I will ride my bike again.

_____

Conventions of grammar, main idea/relevant and irrelevant details, sequence signal words
Directions: If necessary, read the directions for each part. When students have completed the page, present each item and the answer. Correct any errors.

Part 4

Underline the common part. Fill in the circle next to the word that combines the sentences correctly. Combine the sentences with that word.

1. <u>He</u> examined her test.
<u>He</u> gave her an A.
○ and ○ who ○ which

_____

_____

2. <u>The raccoon</u> was alone.
The garbage can was tipped over by <u>the raccoon</u>.
○ and ○ who ○ which

_____

_____

3. The football team <u>drank lots of water</u>.
Their coach <u>drank lots of water</u>.
○ and ○ who ○ which

_____

_____

Part 5

Write what each analogy tells.

• What ending each word has
• What part of speech each word is
• What verb each word comes from
• What each word means

1. Obtainable is to **adjective** as **prediction** is to **noun.**

_____

_____

2. Obtainable is to **obtain** as **prediction** is to **predict.**

_____

_____

3. Obtainable is to **that something can be obtained** as **prediction** is to **a statement that predicts.**

_____

_____

Conventions of grammar/writing sentences, analogies
Directions: If necessary, read the directions for each part. When students have completed the page, present each item and the answer. Correct any errors.

Part 1

Follow the directions.

1. Draw a horizontal line in the box.

2. Place a **b** under the left end of the line.

3. Write a **g** above the right end of the line.

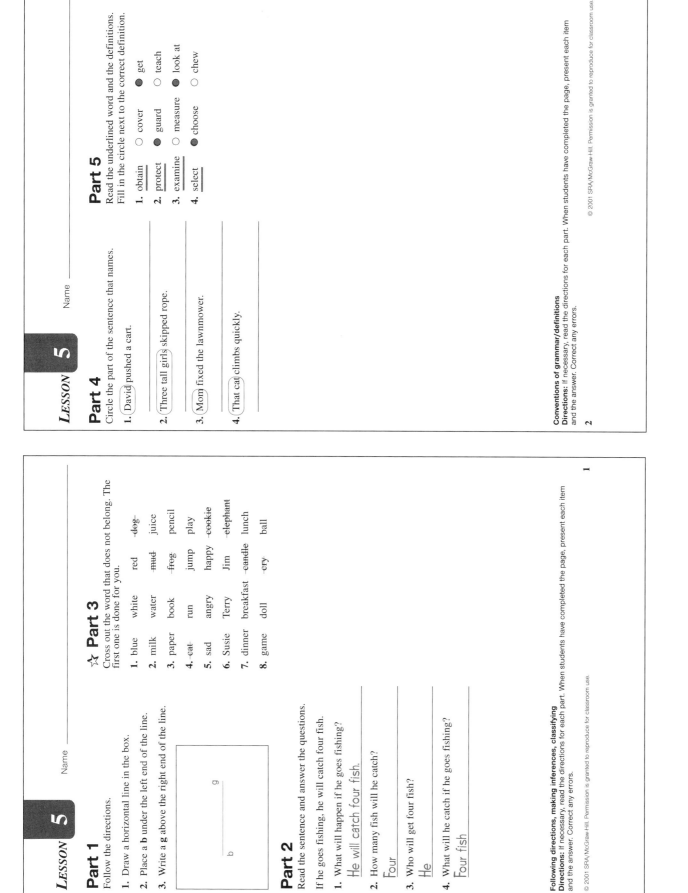

Part 2

Read the sentence and answer the questions.

If he goes fishing, he will catch four fish.

1. What will happen if he goes fishing?

   He will catch four fish.

2. How many fish will he catch?

   Four

3. Who will get four fish?

   He

4. What will he catch if he goes fishing?

   Four fish

☆ Part 3

Cross out the word that does not belong. The first one is done for you.

1. blue   white   red   ~~dog~~

2. milk   water   ~~mud~~   juice

3. paper   book   ~~frog~~   pencil

4. ~~eat~~   run   jump   play

5. sad   angry   happy   ~~cookie~~

6. Susie   Terry   Jim   ~~elephant~~

7. dinner   breakfast   ~~candle~~   lunch

8. game   doll   ~~ery~~   ball

Following directions, making inferences, classifying
Directions: If necessary, read the directions for each part. When students have completed the page, present each item and the answer. Correct any errors.

© 2001 SRA/McGraw-Hill. Permission is granted to reproduce for classroom use.

1

Part 4

Circle the part of the sentence that names.

1. (David) pushed a cart.

2. (Three tall girls) skipped rope.

3. (Mom) fixed the lawnmower.

4. (That cat) climbs quickly.

Part 5

Read the underlined word and the definitions.
Fill in the circle next to the correct definition.

1. obtain   ○ cover   ● get

2. protect   ● guard   ○ teach

3. examine   ○ measure   ● look at

4. select   ● choose   ○ chew

Conventions of grammar/definitions
Directions: If necessary, read the directions for each part. When students have completed the page, present each item and the answer. Correct any errors.

© 2001 SRA/McGraw-Hill. Permission is granted to reproduce for classroom use.

2

113

114

Part 1
Circle the part of the sentence that names.

1. (Jim) ran very fast.
2. (Mark) typed his report.
3. (The dog) jumped on the couch.
4. (Those five ducks) quack loudly.
5. (She) ate her food.

Part 2
Read the sentence and answer the questions.

The skull sits at the top of the spine.

1. Where does the skull sit?
   At the top of the spine

2. Is the skull at the top of the spine?
   Yes

3. What is the skull at the top of?
   The spine

4. What is underneath the skull?
   The spine

☆ Part 3
Read the words in the box. Write each word in the correct group.

dance	red	eat	Andy	blue
green	Lupe	yellow	pink	Jenny
John	write	sing	talk	Dennis

Colors	Names	Actions
red	Andy	dance
blue	Lupe	eat
green	Jenny	write
yellow	John	sing
pink	Dennis	talk

Conventions of grammar, making inferences, classifying
Directions: If necessary, read the directions for each part. When students have completed the page, present each item and the answer. Correct any errors.

Part 4
Follow the directions.

1. Draw a horizontal line in the box.
2. Draw a slanted line under the right end of the horizontal line.
3. Draw a dot above the right end of the horizontal line.

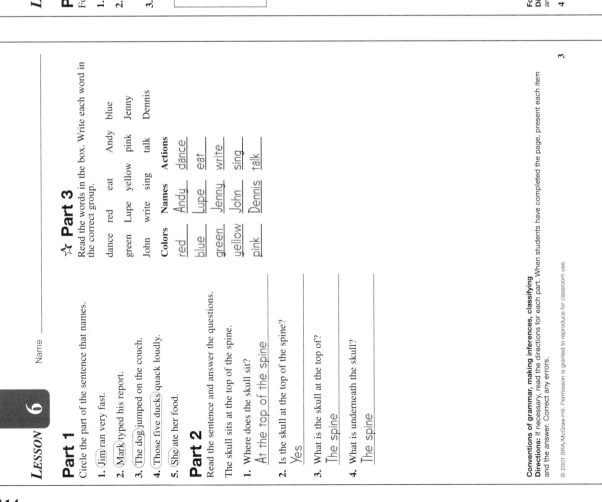

Part 5
Fill in the circle next to the correct form of **obtain** for each of the following sentences.

1. They are _____ new toys.
   ○ obtain   ○ obtained   ● obtaining

2. He _____ new toys.
   ○ obtain   ● obtained   ○ obtaining

3. She will _____ new toys.
   ● obtain   ○ obtained   ○ obtaining

4. I have _____ new toys.
   ○ obtain   ● obtained   ○ obtaining

5. You are _____ new toys.
   ○ obtain   ○ obtained   ● obtaining

Following directions, conventions of grammar
Directions: If necessary, read the directions for each part. When students have completed the page, present each item and the answer. Correct any errors.

Part 1

Read the sentence and answer the questions.

A large glass can hold lots of water.

1. What can hold lots of water?
   A large glass

2. What can a large glass hold?
   Lots of water

3. How much water can a large glass hold?
   Lots

4. What kind of glass can hold lots of water?
   A large glass

Part 2

Follow the directions.

1. Draw a horizontal line.
2. Draw a slanted line above the horizontal line.
3. Draw a vertical line over the slanted line.

or

Part 3

Circle the part of the sentence that names.

1. (The man) waved at a car.
2. (Two boys) waved at the cars.
3. (Jane) sat at a table.
4. (My older brother) stood next to my dad.
5. (One boy) is very happy.
6. (A dog) is an animal.
7. (Dogs) have tails.
8. (Two large dogs) herded the sheep.

☆ Part 4

Circle the thing that does not fit into each category below.

1. Things to play with
   games   dolls   (stores)   balls

2. Things to eat
   potatoes   (lamps)   carrots   apples

3. Parts of a bird
   (hands)   beak   head   wings

Making inferences, following directions, conventions of grammar, classifying
Directions: If necessary, read the directions for each part. When students have completed the page, present each item and the answer. Correct any errors.

5

Part 5

Circle each vehicle. Underline each container.

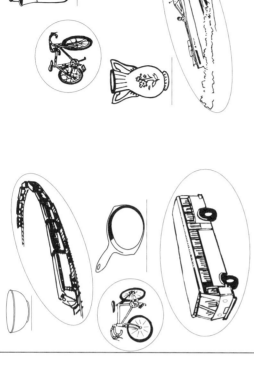

Classification
Directions: If necessary, read the directions for each part. When students have completed the page, present each item and the answer. Correct any errors.

6

116

☆ Part 1

Write the letter that comes next.

1. S T __U__
2. E F __G__
3. K L __M__
4. J K __L__
5. M N __O__

Write the letter that comes in the middle.

6. E __F__ G
7. C __D__ E
8. L __M__ N
9. S __T__ U
10. W __X__ Y

Write the letter that comes before.

11. __A__ B C
12. __K__ L M
13. __R__ S T
14. __E__ F G
15. __J__ K L

Part 2

Write the number of the fact that explains why each thing happened.

1. Beth had a cat.
2. Beth had a hamster.

a. Her pet had a scratching post.   __1__
b. Her pet had an exercise wheel.   __2__
c. Her pet was meowing.   __1__
d. Her pet lived in a cage.   __2__

Part 3

Follow the directions.

1. Draw a horizontal line in the box.
2. Draw a vertical line down from the right end of the horizontal line.
3. Draw a slanted line from the bottom of the vertical line to the left end of the horizontal line.

7

Part 4

Underline the part of the sentence that names.

1. That bus was moving very slowly.
2. A tired bird flew to a branch.
3. Tara got mad at Joey.
4. The wagon was blue.
5. The holiday lights look pretty at night.
6. My older brother has a new game.
7. Cats like to play with string.
8. The shiny new car hit a light pole.

Part 5

Underline each container.

Cross out each vehicle.

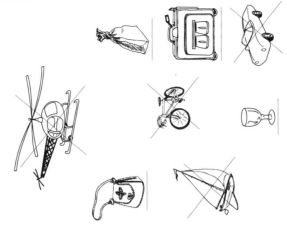

☆ Part 1

Number the words in **ABC order.** Then write the words in the right order.

1. 2 ball   1. apple
   1 apple   2. ball
   3 car   3. car

2. 1 dog   1. dog
   3 fish   2. egg
   2 egg   3. fish

3. 3 pan   1. nail
   1 nail   2. oak
   2 oak   3. pan

Part 2

Write a word that comes from **protect** in each blank.

1. The boy was protecting the fort.

2. That lock will protect my locker.

3. Those gloves had protected her hands.

4. Gary had a helmet to protect his head.

Part 3

Write **ribs, skull,** or **spine** in each blank.

1. ribs
2. spine
3. skull

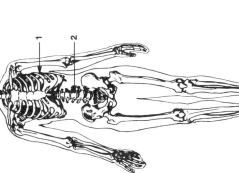

Alphabetical order, inflectional suffixes, graphic aids
Directions: If necessary, read the directions for each part. When students have completed the page, present each item and the answer. Correct any errors.

9

Part 4

Underline the part of each sentence that names. Then circle the noun in that part.

1. The (class) lasted a short time.
2. My (dad) has a new suit.
3. That old white (cat) is very tired.
4. His (mom) worked very well.
5. That (cat) was a kitten.
6. (Nigel) wrote a fantastic story.
7. This grumpy (baby) frowns a lot.
8. (Cars) can't park in this space.

Part 5

Write the number of the fact that explains why each thing happened.

1. **The weather was wet.**
2. **The weather was dry.**

a. The man slipped.   1
b. The boy drank a lot of water.   2
c. The woman wore a raincoat.   1
d. They had a lot of trouble starting the campfire.   1

Part 6

Follow the directions.

1. Draw a slanted line down to the left.
2. Draw a vertical line down from the top end of the slanted line.
3. Draw a slanted line from the bottom of the vertical line up to the right.

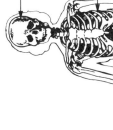

Conventions of grammar, drawing conclusions based on evidence, following directions
Directions: If necessary, read the directions for each part. When students have completed the page, present each item and the answer. Correct any errors.

10

LESSON 10

Name _____

☆ Part 1
Write each set of words in **ABC order.**

| soap   dream   east |

1. dream
2. east
3. soap

| trip   week   road |

1. road
2. trip
3. week

Part 2
Write a word that comes from **examine** in each blank.

1. A doctor will _examine_ my throat.
2. That dentist had _examined_ Tim's teeth.
3. Six policemen are _examining_ that old building.
4. This scientist wants to _examine_ Barbara's rock.
5. A baker will _examine_ this cake.

Part 3
Underline the part that names and circle the verb in each sentence.

1. Jake (walked) all day.
2. Her dad (drove) a new car.
3. Her dad (was driving) a new car.
4. Her dad (was washing) the car.
5. That girl (painted) a fence.
6. My mother (was baking) in the kitchen.
7. Robert (went) to the kitchen.
8. The dog (slid) across the floor.

Alphabetical order, inflectional suffixes, conventions of grammar
Directions: If necessary, read the directions for each part. When students have completed the page, present each item and the answer. Correct any errors.

11

LESSON 10

Name _____

Part 4
Write **ribs**, **skull**, or **spine** in each blank.

1. spine
2. skull
3. ribs

Part 5
Follow the directions.

1. Draw a horizontal line in the box.
2. Draw a vertical line down from the left end of the horizontal line.
3. Write a **7** on the right side of the vertical line.

Part 6
Read the sentence and answer the questions.

> **Those birds will make their nest in a tree or on a building ledge.**

1. Where will they make their nest?
   In a tree or on a building ledge
2. Will they make their nest in a tree and a building ledge?
   No
3. Will they make their nest in a tree or on a building ledge?
   Yes
4. What word tells whose nest the birds will make?
   Their

Graphic aids, following directions, making inferences
Directions: If necessary, read the directions for each part. When students have completed the page, present each item and the answer. Correct any errors.

12

Name _____

Part 1

Follow the directions.

1. Draw a vertical line in the box.

2. Draw a line that slants down to the left from the top of the vertical line.

3. Draw a line that slants down to the right from the top of the vertical line.

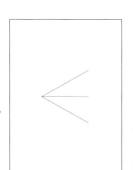

Part 2

Circle the word in each part that names. Make a box around the verb in each sentence.

1. The (kids) were producing a play.

2. The (kids) bought clothes for costumes.

3. Six (girls) were climbing that tree.

4. A white (cat) walked along the fence.

5. The (boys) swam in the creek.

6. My (brother) is swimming in the creek.

Part 3

Write the number of the fact that explains why each thing happened.

1. Jessie has a sore hip.
2. Kelly broke her humerus.

a. She has a cast on her arm.   2

b. A doctor examined her pelvis.   1

c. She has trouble going up stairs.   1

d. She has to write with her other hand.   2

Part 4

Write a word that comes from **obtain** in each blank.

1. She is ___obtaining___ a piece of pie.

2. Eric wants to ___obtain___ a broom from this store.

3. He has ___obtained___ a football from this store.

4. They are ___obtaining___ gold and silver from this mine.

5. Mac has ___obtained___ blue suspenders for his pants.

Following directions, conventions of grammar, drawing conclusions based on evidence, inflectional suffixes
Directions: If necessary, read the directions for each part. When students have completed the page, present each item and the answer. Correct any errors.

© 2001 SRA/McGraw-Hill. Permission is granted to reproduce for classroom use.   13

☆ Part 5

Words that mean the same or nearly the same are called **synonyms.**
Examples:
sleep-rest   cold-chilly

Read each sentence below. Find a synonym from the box for each underlined word. Write the word on the line.

| home | sick | small |
| dad | gift | yelled |

1. Tim gave me a <u>present</u> for my birthday.
   gift

2. I saw a <u>little</u> kitten in our yard.
   small

3. My <u>house</u> is on a corner.
   home

4. I almost fell <u>ill</u>.
   sick

5. Dave <u>shouted</u> for me to go.
   yelled

6. My <u>father</u> travels a lot.
   dad

Part 6

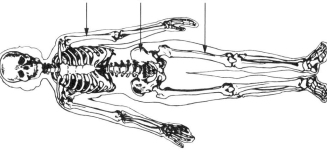

Write **humerus, femur,** or **pelvis** in each blank.

1. humerus

2. femur

3. pelvis

Synonyms, graphic aids
Directions: If necessary, read the directions for each part. When students have completed the page, present each item and the answer. Correct any errors.

14   © 2001 SRA/McGraw-Hill. Permission is granted to reproduce for classroom use.

120

Part 1

Underline the verbs.

1. A young girl protects her doll.

2. A woman protects the gold in that chest.

3. Her friend constructs chests and his pal selects games.

4. His friend constructs chests and selects games.

5. His little sister scuffed her shoe.

6. She cleaned off the scuff quickly.

☆ Part 2

Choose a synonym in ( ) for the underlined word.

1. The test was simple. (hard, easy)

   easy

2. Cody likes doing tricks. (hates, enjoys)

   enjoys

3. We watched the basketball player jump into the air. (leap, crawl)

   leap

4. The ladder is by the back door. (rear, front)

   rear

Part 3

Write **femur, humerus, pelvis, ribs, skull,** or **spine** in each blank.

1. pelvis

2. ribs

3. spine

4. femur

5. skull

6. humerus

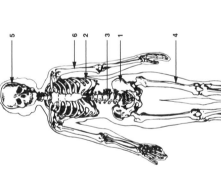

Conventions of grammar/verbs, synonyms, graphic aids
Directions: If necessary, read the directions for each part. When students have completed the page, present each item and the answer. Correct any errors.

© 2001 SRA/McGraw-Hill. Permission is granted to reproduce for classroom use.

Part 4

Write a word that comes from **construct** in each blank.

1. Mom wants to ___construct___ a boat.

2. Those men are planning to ___construct___ a house.

3. Her aunt is ___constructing___ a garage.

4. That boy has ___constructed___ a wooden scooter.

5. You cannot ___construct___ a slide with sand.

Part 6

Follow the directions.

1. Draw a vertical line in the box.

2. Draw two horizontal lines to the right of the vertical line.

3. Write a **q** at the bottom end of the vertical line.

Part 7

Circle the noun in each part. Underline the verb in each sentence.

1. (Jan) threw a football.

2. Many (ducks) were eating from the bird feeder.

3. His (sister) tripped on the curb.

4. Four small (chipmunks) were squeaking at Jim.

5. That (girl) eats lunch at noon.

6. Their (father) is building some stairs.

Part 5

Write the number of the fact that explains why each thing happened.

1. **Warren was hot.**
2. **Gil was cold.**

a. He was sweating.   1

b. He was fanning himself.   1

c. He was shivering.   2

d. He made hot chocolate.   2

Inflectional suffixes, drawing conclusions based on evidence, following directions, conventions of grammar
Directions: If necessary, read the directions for each part. When students have completed the page, present each item and the answer. Correct any errors.

16

© 2001 SRA/McGraw-Hill. Permission is granted to reproduce for classroom use.

Part 1

For each numbered word, write the letter of the word's definition.

1. construct — g   a. (v.) guard
2. examine — i   b. (n.) the bone that covers the brain
3. obtain — d   c. (n.) a word that tells the actions that things do
4. protect — a   d. (v.) get
5. ribs — h   e. (v.) choose
6. select — e   f. (n.) the backbone
7. skeletal system — j   g. (v.) build
8. skull — b   h. (n.) the bones that cover the organs in the chest
9. spine — f   i. (v.) look at
10. verb — c   j. (n.) the body system of bones

Part 2

Write the number of the fact that explains why each thing happened.

1. **Joe said, "Buy."**
2. **Tom said, "Horse."**

a. He said what to do.   1
b. He said a verb.   1
c. He said a noun.   2
d. The thing he said was an animal.   2

Definitions, drawing conclusions based on evidence
Directions: If necessary, read the directions for each part. When students have completed the page, present each item and the answer. Correct any errors.

☆ Part 3

Use the words in the box below to write a synonym for each word.

road	cap	begin	hike
correct	happy	under	close

1. walk   hike
2. start   begin
3. glad   happy
4. hat   cap
5. shut   close
6. below   under
7. street   road
8. right   correct

Part 4

Write a word that comes from **select** in each blank.

1. Nancy has _selected_ a dog for her family.
2. Scott will _select_ a computer for his office.
3. Jon was _selected_ by the teacher.
4. The woman is _selecting_ a skirt at the mall.

Part 5

Follow the directions.

1. Write a **Y** in the box.
2. Draw three horizontal lines to the right of the **Y**.
3. Write a **3** to the left of the **Y**.

Synonyms, inflectional suffixes, following directions
Directions: If necessary, read the directions for each part. When students have completed the page, present each item and the answer. Correct any errors.

121

LESSON 14

Name _____

Part 1

Underline both nouns in each sentence.

1. The boy ran from the park.
2. My father stood over that hole.
3. The woman drank the soda slowly.
4. David scanned the newspaper quickly.
5. My sister likes the circus.
6. Not many people live in Alaska.

Part 2

Read the sentence and answer the questions.

> A carpenter has to construct lots of floors for new houses.

1. Who has to construct floors?
   A carpenter

2. What kind of houses does a carpenter construct floors for?
   New

3. Does a carpenter build floors for houses?
   Yes

4. How many floors does a carpenter construct?
   Lots

☆ Part 3

> Words that mean the opposite are called **antonyms.**
> **Examples:**
> up-down   day-night

Draw a line to the antonym for each underlined word.

1. a high <u>bridge</u>   soft

2. a <u>sad</u> movie   dark

3. <u>off</u> the table   happy

4. a <u>light</u> color   long

5. a <u>short</u> story   on

6. a <u>hard</u> bed   low

LESSON 14

Name _____

Part 4

Write **skull, ribs, femur, humerus, spine,** or **pelvis** in each blank.

1. femur
2. skull
3. humerus
4. spine
5. pelvis
6. ribs

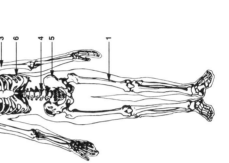

Part 5

Write a word that comes from **protect** in each blank.

1. The boot is <u>protecting</u> his foot.
2. That yard was <u>protected</u> by a fence.
3. The police <u>protect</u> you.
4. Your heart is <u>protected</u> by your ribs.
5. The shack was <u>protecting</u> us from the rain.

Part 6

Circle the noun in each part. Underline the verb in each sentence.

1. The (girl) was running in the street.
2. The (girls) were running in the street.
3. The (girls) lived on a wide street.
4. This (night) is very cool.
5. Last (night) was cooler.
6. The (grass) feels cool.

LESSON 15

Name _____

Part 1

Fill in each blank.

1. skull
2. spine
3. pelvis
4. humerus
5. ribs
6. femur

Part 2

Break the code. Fill in each blank. Then do what the sentence tells you to do.

Make	a	circle
snay	q	cru
under	the	line
m	flep	ret

q = a
flep = the
cru = circle
snay = make
m = under
ret = line

◯

Part 3

Underline each noun in the sentences. Circle each verb.

1. The train (had) a bent wheel.
2. His new hat (was sitting) on the table.
3. Joe (sold) old video games.
4. The young lion (was running).
5. Our town (constructed) a new school.
6. Three girls and three boys (played) in the ocean.

Graphic aids, following directions, conventions of grammar
Directions: If necessary, read the directions for each part. When students have completed the page, present each item and the answer. Correct any errors.

21

LESSON 15

Name _____

☆ Part 4

Choose an antonym in ( ) for the underlined word.

1. The student will answer either yes or ____.
   no
   (maybe, no)

2. When food isn't good, it's ____.
   bad
   (hot, bad)

3. Summer is hot, and winter is ____.
   cold
   (snow, cold)

4. I like to run fast, not ____.
   slow
   (slow, far)

Part 5

Underline each noun in the sentences.

1. Marla doesn't like Tom as well as Matt.
2. A little girl walked on the couch.
3. My mom was washing the floor.
4. My brother kept his candy under his pillow.
5. Westin dropped a penny in the sewer.

Part 6

Read the sentence and answer the questions.

> The woman cracked her femur when she tripped on the sidewalk.

1. When did the woman crack her femur?
   When she tripped on the sidewalk

2. What bone did the woman break?
   Her femur

3. Where did the woman trip?
   On the sidewalk

4. What did the woman do to her femur?
   Cracked it

5. Who broke her femur?
   The woman

Antonyms, conventions of grammar, making inferences
Directions: If necessary, read the directions for each part. When students have completed the page, present each item and the answer. Correct any errors.

22

124

LESSON 16

Name _____

Part 1

Break the code. Fill in each blank. Then do what the sentence tells you to do.

Make	a		box
jik	di		mij
over	the		line
nort	bac		fase

jik = make
mij = box
fase = line
nort = over
bac = the
di = a

Part 2

Write a word that comes from **construct** in each blank.

1. The farmers have __constructed__ a large pig pen.

2. These toys were __constructed__ by hand.

3. That deck was __constructed__ by her dad.

4. Those wasps will __construct__ a hive.

5. The man is __constructing__ a doghouse for his dog.

☆ Part 3

Read the words. Write **S** if the underlined words are synonyms. Write **A** if they are antonyms.

1. __A__ old hat, new hat
2. __S__ fast bike, quick bike
3. __S__ large dog, big dog
4. __A__ first day, last day
5. __A__ cold drink, hot drink

Part 4

Circle each verb in the sentences.

1. The new car was running smoothly.
2. Some boys found a frog.
3. The cat purred and rolled over.
4. Don lost his balance and fell off the wall.
5. The man dug a ditch and sat on the edge.
6. Jill drank water and rubbed her arm.
7. Tony bought dinner and went home.
8. The clowns were chasing the dogs.

Following directions, inflectional suffixes, antonyms/synonyms, conventions of grammar
Directions: If necessary, read the directions for each part. When students have completed the page, present each item and the answer. Correct any errors.

© 2001 SRA/McGraw-Hill. Permission is granted to reproduce for classroom use.

23

LESSON 16

Name _____

Part 5

Circle each container.
Cross out each living thing.
Underline each piece of clothing.

Part 6

Fill in each blank.

1. __skull__
2. __humerus__
3. __ribs__
4. __spine__
5. __pelvis__
6. __femur__

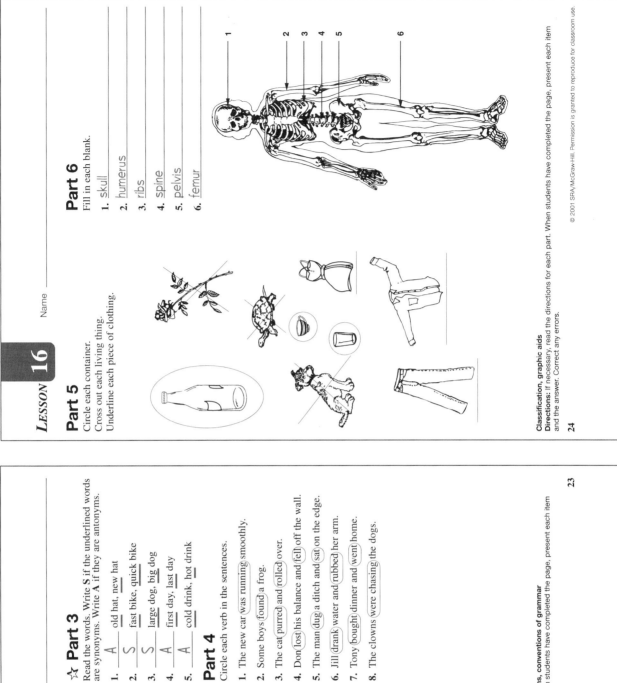

Classification, graphic aids
Directions: If necessary, read the directions for each part. When students have completed the page, present each item and the answer. Correct any errors.

24　　　© 2001 SRA/McGraw-Hill. Permission is granted to reproduce for classroom use.

Part 1

Break the code. Fill in each blank. Then do what the sentence tells you to do.

write	the	word
falg	ga	berp
femur	under	the
por	h	diw
line		
xuh		

ga = the
xuh = line
berp = word
por = femur
diw = the
falg = write
h = under

Part 2

1. Jake fell out of a tree.
2. A doctor took care of Jake.

Write the number of the fact that explains why each thing happened.

a. His ankle was broken.

b. He lost his balance and fell.

c. He landed hard.

d. He put a cast on his foot.

_____
_____
_____
_2_

Part 3

Fill in each blank.

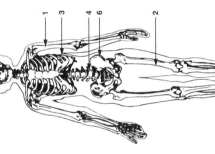

1. humerus
2. femur
3. ribs
4. spine
5. skull
6. pelvis

Following directions, draw conclusions based on evidence, graphic aids
Directions: If necessary, read the directions for each part. When students have completed the page, present each item and the answer. Correct any errors.

☆ Part 4

Some sentences are statements. They tell something.
The Grand Canyon is in Arizona.

Some sentences are questions. They ask something.
Is the Grand Canyon in Arizona?

Write **S** in front of each statement.
Write **Q** in front of each question.

S   Sue ate fried chicken.

Q   Did Sarah find the rolls?

Q   Is he hungry?

S   We walked to the park.

S   Marcia left for her trip.

Q   Did he get sick and leave?

S   Steve wanted to see the plane.

Q   Is Max ready to go?

S   This was a long week.

Q   Will you give me one?

Part 5

Complete the deductions.

1. Every dog is a mammal.
   Roscoe is a dog.
   So, Roscoe is a mammal.

2. All girls are persons.
   Gwen is a girl.
   So, Gwen is a person.

3. All of the Smiths are football fans.
   Terry's last name is Smith.
   So, Terry is a football fan.

4. All birds have feathers.
   A penguin is a bird.
   So, a penguin has feathers.

5. All nuts have a shell.
   A buckeye is a nut.
   So, a buckeye has a shell.

Types of sentences, deductions
Directions: If necessary, read the directions for each part. When students have completed the page, present each item and the answer. Correct any errors.

126

Part 1

Complete the deductions.

1. Kory has every video game.
   "Blitz" is a video game.
   So, Kory has "Blitz."

2. Andy likes all sweets.
   Bubble gum is sweet.
   So, Andy likes bubble gum.

3. Fish can breathe under water.
   A trout is a fish.
   So, a trout can breathe under water.

4. Paper is made from tree pulp.
   You're writing on paper.
   So, you're writing on tree pulp.

4. What do dogs eat?
   Meat

5. Do dogs eat meat and plants?
   No

☆ Part 3

| Some sentences are commands. They tell somebody to do something. _Please set the table._ |
| Some sentences are exclamations. They show strong feelings or surprise. _What a wonderful trip!_ |

Write **C** in front of each command.
Write **E** in front of each exclamation.

E   What a great time we'll have!
C   Add the eggs to the batter.
C   Watch out for that ladder.
C   Brush your teeth first.
E   The dog ate the hamburger!
E   I am so happy!
C   Pass the salt, please.
C   Clean the sink well.
C   Slice the apples.
E   What a cute puppy!

Part 2

Read the sentence in the box and answer the questions.

| Dogs eat meat and deer eat plants. |

1. Which kind of animal eats meat?
   Dogs

2. Which kind of animal eats plants?
   Deer

3. Do deer eat meat and plants?
   No

Deductions, making inferences, types of sentences
Directions: If necessary, read the directions for each part. When students have completed the page, present each item and the answer. Correct any errors.

27

Part 5

For each numbered word, write the letter of the word's definition.

1. construct	c	a. (v.) choose
2. examine	f	b. (v.) get
3. femur	i	c. (v.) build
4. humerus	d	d. (n.) the upper arm bone
5. noun	h	e. (n.) the hip bone
6. obtain	b	f. (v.) look at
7. pelvis	e	g. (v.) guard
8. protect	g	h. (n.) a word that names a person, place, or thing
9. select	a	i. (n.) the upper leg bone
10. verb	j	j. (n.) a word that tells the action that things do

Definitions
Directions: If necessary, read the directions for each part. When students have completed the page, present each item and the answer. Correct any errors.

28

☆ Part 1

Put a period (.) at the end of a statement.
Pat is my friend.

Put a question mark (?) at the end of a question.
Where did she go?

Put an exclamation mark (!) at the end of an exclamation.
Watch out!

Put a period (.) at the end of a command.
Turn off the water.

Read each sentence and put the correct punctuation mark at the end.

1. We are in school today .
2. He has a younger sister .
3. It's snowing really hard !
4. Is that your bike ?
5. It's so cold today !
6. Let's walk to the movie .

Part 2

Write a word that comes from **protect** in each blank. Then fill in the circle next to **verb, noun,** or **adjective.**

1. The _protective_ dog scared the intruder.
   ○ verb ○ noun ● adjective
2. The cheetah had to _protect_ her cubs.
   ● verb ○ noun ○ adjective
3. Insurance policies provide _protection_ against loss from theft, fire, and floods.
   ○ verb ● noun ○ adjective

Part 3

Write the number of the fact that explains why each thing happened.

1. **Lonnie got an old rookie baseball card.**
2. **Sam found a green rock.**

a. It cost him a lot.   1
b. He will show it to his science class.   2
c. He will keep it in a special folder.   1
d. He is careful not to drop it on his foot.   2

Part 4

Follow the directions.

1. Draw a horizontal line from the left side of the box to the right side of the box.
2. Draw a circle underneath the horizontal line.
3. Draw three vertical lines above the horizontal line.

Part 5

Complete the deductions.

1. Jon does not have anything made of leather.
   Baseball gloves are made of leather.
   So, Jon does not have a
   baseball glove.
2. Teachers are smart people.
   Megan is a teacher.
   So, Megan is a
   smart person.

Part 6

Circle the verbs. Underline the nouns.

1. Broken glass (is) not safe.
2. Mom (is going) to a recital.
3. The man (baked) pies.
4. Barb (welded) pipes and (drove) nails.
5. Seth and John (love) their pool.
6. Lee (knew) Kay's aunt and uncle.

LESSON 20   Name _____

Part 1

Read the story and answer the questions.

> Kelvin's back hurt, so he went to a doctor. The doctor said, "You've been lifting lots and lots of heavy boxes. If you don't take a break, you could hurt your back forever."

1. Why did Kelvin go to a doctor?
   His back hurt.

2. How many boxes did Kelvin lift?
   Lots and lots

3. What will happen if Kelvin doesn't take a break?
   He could hurt his back forever.

4. How could Kelvin hurt his back forever?
   By not taking a break

☆ Part 2

> Names of the days of the week begin with a capital letter.
> **Examples:** Sunday, Monday, Friday
>
> Abbreviations of the days of the week begin with a capital letter.
> **Examples:** Sun., Mon., Tues., Wed., Thurs., Fri., Sat.

Write the days of the week to complete each sentence.

1. The first day of the week is
   Sunday

2. The day that comes before Sunday is
   Saturday

3. The day in the middle of the week is
   Wednesday

Write the correct abbreviation for the day of the week.

Sunday	Sun.
Monday	Mon.
Tuesday	Tues.
Wednesday	Wed.
Thursday	Thurs.
Friday	Fri.
Saturday	Sat.

LESSON 20   Name _____

Part 3

Complete the analogy by filling in the circle next to the best choice.

A **monkey** is to **climbing**

1. as a dolphin is to
   - ○ crawling
   - ● swimming

2. as a kangaroo is to
   - ○ running
   - ● hopping

3. as a tiger is to
   - ○ swimming
   - ● running

Part 4

Complete the deductions.

1. Fred did not have any pets.
   A hamster is a pet.
   So, Fred did not have
   a hamster.

2. An adjective is a word that describes something.
   Interesting is an adjective.
   So, interesting describes
   something.

Part 5

Write the number of the fact that explains why each thing happened.

1. **Kyle said, "Obtain."**
2. **Tom said, "Construction."**

a. He said a verb. ___1___

b. He said a noun. ___2___

c. He was talking about something that is built. ___2___

d. He was talking about getting something. ___1___

Part 6

Draw a line over each adjective.

1. Many fish need salt water.

2. Big cars are hard to drive.

3. The bright sun helped the plants grow.

4. Small dogs bark more than big dogs.

5. My sister is a very pretty girl.

6. Jasper, where is your green shirt?

Part 1

Write **esophagus**, **mouth**, or **stomach** in each blank.

1. esophagus
2. stomach
3. mouth

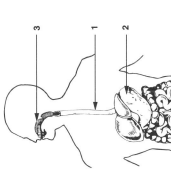

Part 2

Fill in each blank with the word that has the same meaning as the word or words under the blank.

| examine | protecting |
| select | constructed |

1. He told her to __examine__ six problems.
   (look at)

2. Those dogs are __protecting__ that house.
   (guarding)

3. The boy was allowed to __select__ one puppy.
   (choose)

4. Who __constructed__ that tree house?
   (built)

Part 3

Complete the analogy by filling in the circle next to the best choice.

A **tongue** is to **tasting**

1. as **feet** are to ___.
   ○ hearing ○ seeing ● running

2. as **eyes** are to ___.
   ○ hearing ● seeing ○ running

3. as **ears** are to ___.
   ● hearing ○ seeing ○ running

Graphic aids, vocabulary, analogies
Directions: If necessary, read the directions for each part. When students have completed the page, present each item and the answer. Correct any errors.

© 2001 SRA/McGraw-Hill. Permission is granted to reproduce for classroom use.

33

Part 4

Circle the verbs. Underline the nouns.

1. That dog was standing on the rug.
2. Those women were lawyers.
3. His dog has eaten.
4. That cop is a woman.
5. Four cats are on the fence.
6. Those boys were playing.

Part 5

Fill in each blank. Then do what the sentence tells you to do.

make   a   horizontal
graz   pulg   pim

line   over   the
dok   kur   gurb

K
dilk

pulg = a
kur = over
graz = make
gurb = the
dilk = K
pim = horizontal
dok = line

☆ Part 6

• Names of the months begin with a capital letter.
• The abbreviations of the months end with a period.
  Examples: Jan., Feb., Mar., Dec.

Write the names of the months correctly.

1. january — January
2. february — February
3. march — March
4. april — April
5. may — May
6. june — June
7. july — July
8. august — August
9. september — September
10. october — October
11. november — November
12. december — December

Conventions of grammar, following directions, capitalization
Directions: If necessary, read the directions for each part. When students have completed the page, present each item and the answer. Correct any errors.

© 2001 SRA/McGraw-Hill. Permission is granted to reproduce for classroom use.

34

130

☆ Part 1

- Each word in the name of a holiday begins with a **capital letter.**
  Examples:
  Memorial Day Labor Day

Write the holiday names correctly.

1. new year's day
   New Year's Day

2. thanksgiving day
   Thanksgiving Day

3. independence day
   Independence Day

4. valentine's day
   Valentine's Day

5. father's day
   Father's Day

6. martin luther king, jr. day
   Martin Luther King, Jr. Day

Part 2

Complete the analogy.

Examine is to **look** at

1. as **select** is to ____choose____.

2. as **protect** is to ____guard____.

3. as **obtain** is to ____get____.

Part 3

Use the words in the box to complete the sentences.

| constructed | obtained |
| protect | selecting |

1. Their security system was selected to ____protect____ that house.
   (guard)

2. A fisherman ____constructed____ some lobster traps.
   (built)

3. He ____obtained____ some tools for his brother. (got)

4. They are ____selecting____ a school for him to attend. (choosing)

35

Capitalization, conventions of grammar/verbs, analogies, vocabulary
Directions: If necessary, read the directions for each part. When students have completed the page, present each item and the answer. Correct any errors.

© 2001 SRA/McGraw-Hill. Permission is granted to reproduce for classroom use.

Part 4

Write **mouth**, **esophagus**, or **stomach** in each blank.

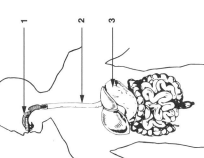

1. mouth

2. esophagus

3. stomach

Part 5

Read the story and answer the questions.

Zach wanted to clean his clothes, so he threw them over a clothesline in the backyard. "You can't wash your clothes on a clothesline," his dad said, "but you can dry them on the line after you wash them." So Zach washed his clothes in the sink, then hung them on the clothesline to dry.

1. Did Zach use the sink at first?
   No

2. When did Zach use the sink?
   After his dad told
   him to

3. When can you use a clothesline?
   After you wash your
   clothes

4. Did Zach wash or dry the clothes first?
   He dried them.

5. Who told Zach he couldn't use the clothesline first? His dad

36

Graphic aids, making inferences
Directions: If necessary, read the directions for each part. When students have completed the page, present each item and the answer. Correct any errors.

© 2001 SRA/McGraw-Hill. Permission is granted to reproduce for classroom use.

Part 1

For each numbered word or phrase write the letter of its definition.

a. (n.) something that protects
b. (n.) a word that comes before a noun and tells about the noun
c. (v.) choose
d. (v.) build
e. (v.) get
f. (n.) the organ that mixes food with chemicals
g. (a.) that something protects
h. (n.) the body system that changes food into fuel
i. (n.) the tube that goes from the mouth to the stomach
j. (n.) the part that takes in solid and liquid food

1. adjective __b__
2. construct __d__
3. digestive system __h__
4. esophagus __i__
5. mouth __j__
6. obtain __e__
7. protection __a__
8. protective __g__
9. select __c__
10. stomach __f__

Part 2

Follow the directions.

1. Draw a horizontal line.

2. Draw a line that slants down to the left from the left end of the horizontal line.

3. Draw a line from the bottom of the slanted line to the right end of the horizontal line.

Part 3

Read the story and answer the questions.

> It was snowing, and Jenny wanted to use her new sled. She took her sled to her backyard and sat down on it, but the sled didn't move. Her mom said, "You need a steep hill. The steeper the hill, the better the sled will slide."

1. What did Jenny want to use?
   Her new sled

2. What will happen if Jenny finds a steeper hill?
   The sled will slide better.

3. Will the sled slide better on a steep hill or in a flat yard?
   On a steep hill

4. What kind of hill will make the sled slide?
   A steep hill

5. If Jenny finds a steep hill, what will the sled do?
   Slide better

☆ Part 4

- A **contraction** is a word made by joining two words.
- An **apostrophe** (') shows where a letter or letters are left out.

  Examples:
  do not = don't   is not = isn't
  can not = can't   are not = aren't

Draw a line from the two words to the contraction.

1. was not — hasn't
2. were not — didn't
3. did not — aren't
4. has not — haven't
5. are not — weren't
6. have not — wasn't

Write each contraction as two words.

7. don't   do   not
8. can't   can not
9. hadn't   had not
10. isn't   is   not

131

132

Part 1

Underline the nouns. Draw a line over the adjectives.

1. His friend ate on the dock.
2. The woman rode her bike down trails.
3. A rap group will play in our city.
4. A blue envelope is in the doorway.
5. Her mom and her brother were sitting on rocks.
6. That truck is in a narrow alley.
7. Two sharks ate fast fish and green eels.
8. Her father read in the shaded hammock.

Part 2

Complete the analogy.

A spine is to a back

1. as a pelvis is to a _____ hip _____.
2. as a femur is to a _____ leg _____.
3. as a humerus is to an _____ arm _____.

Part 3

Write small intestine, large intestine, or liver in each blank.

1. small intestine
2. large intestine
3. liver

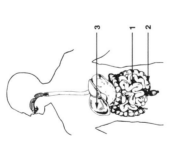

© 2001 SRA/McGraw-Hill. Permission is granted to reproduce for classroom use.

Conventions of grammar, analogies, graphic aids
Directions: If necessary, read the directions for each part. When students have completed the page, present each item and the answer. Correct any errors.

39

Part 4

Read the story and answer the questions.

A young boy liked candy more than fruit. His doctor told him, "Candy is bad for your digestive system. You should eat fruit. The more fruit you eat, the better you will feel." So the young boy ate fruit, but he would reward himself with candy when he got good grades in school.

1. What did the young boy like more than fruit?
   Candy
2. What did the doctor tell him to eat?
   Fruit
3. What will happen if the boy eats more fruit?
   He will feel better.
4. When did he eat candy? When he got good grades
5. If he wants to feel better, what will he do?
   Eat fruit

☆Part 5

Underline each contraction.

1. Let's eat something now.
2. They can't see everything.
3. We'll wait outside for you.
4. Doesn't it seem like spring today?
5. I wish he wasn't going to the city.

Part 6

Follow the directions.

1. Draw a vertical line.
2. Write a J at the top end of the vertical line.
3. Write a K at the bottom end of the vertical line.
4. Write a D to the left of the vertical line.

Making inferences, contractions, following directions
Directions: If necessary, read the directions for each part. When students have completed the page, present each item and the answer. Correct any errors.

40   © 2001 SRA/McGraw-Hill. Permission is granted to reproduce for classroom use.

LESSON 25

Name _____

Part 1

Write **stomach, mouth, liver, esophagus, large intestine,** or **small intestine** in each blank.

1. stomach
2. large intestine
3. esophagus
4. mouth
5. liver
6. small intestine

41

Part 2

Write a word that comes from **obtain** or **construct** in each blank. Then fill in the circle next to **verb, noun,** or **adjective.**

1. An old man will _____obtain_____ a pair of slippers from the store.
   ● verb ○ noun ○ adjective

2. Those __constructive__ twins make the most of their time.
   ○ verb ○ noun ● adjective

3. There will be a lot of __construction__ downtown this summer.
   ○ verb ● noun ○ adjective

4. I'll bet he __obtained__ those diamonds illegally.
   ● verb ○ noun ○ adjective

5. The __construction__ will be off-limits to children.
   ○ verb ● noun ○ adjective

Part 3

Complete the analogy.

A **noun** is to **parts of speech**

1. as a **lion** is to _____animals_____ .
2. as a **bus** is to _____vehicles_____ .
3. as a **fern** is to _____plants_____ .

LESSON 25

Name _____

Part 4

Read the sentences and answer the questions. Circle **W** after each question that is answered by words in the sentences, and underline those words. Circle **D** after each question that is answered by a deduction.

1. **Every person has a stomach.**
2. **Carla is a person.**

a. What does every person have?
   A stomach _____ Ⓦ D

b. Does Carla have a stomach?
   Yes _____ W Ⓓ

c. Does Carla have a digestive system?
   Yes _____ W Ⓓ

d. Is Carla a person? Yes _____ Ⓦ D

Part 5

Circle the verbs. Underline the nouns.

1. A small man (cut) flowers.
2. Four pandas (live) at the animal refuge.
3. Her dad (is) an engineer.
4. Many people (enjoy) baseball and football.

☆ Part 6

Write a **contraction** for the two words in parentheses.

1. I (do not) _____don't_____ have my lunch today.

2. My friends (were not) __weren't__ in the gym.

3. Mary (is not) __isn't__ planning on going to camp.

4. (Did not) __Didn't__ you put the dog out this morning?

5. Her parents (are not) __aren't__ moving.

6. I (can not) __can't__ figure out this problem.

7. Jane and Tracy (have not) __haven't__ been to New York City.

133

Part 1

Make each sentence begin with a capital letter. Put the correct punctuation mark at the end of each sentence.

1. I'm very excited that my grandparents are coming.
2. I'd like to examine your baseball card collection.
3. Tony enjoyed throwing darts with Pete.
4. Could you help me with this math problem?
5. Has anyone seen my shoes?

Part 2

Fill in each blank. Then do what the sentence tells you to do.

shade	in	the	45
right	98		
32	oval	54	

45 = the
54 = oval
67 = shade
98 = in
32 = right

Part 3

Read the sentences and answer the questions. Circle **W** after each question that is answered by words in the sentences, and underline those words. Circle **D** after each question that is answered by a deduction.

Some words are adjectives. *Snappy* **is a word.**

1. Is **snappy** an adjective?
   Maybe   W (D)
2. What are some words?
   Adjectives   (W) D
3. How many words are adjectives?
   Some   W (D)
4. Does **snappy** describe a noun?
   Maybe   (W) D

Part 4

Underline the nouns. Draw a line over the adjectives. Circle the verbs.

1. Those two men cut four small trees.
2. Kathy and her sister enjoy fishing with their mom.
3. Skiing is a fun activity.

Part 5

Write a word that comes from **examine** or **select** in each blank. Then fill in the circle next to **verb, noun,** or **adjective.**

1. A nurse will examine Kristi's feet.
   ● verb ○ noun ○ adjective
2. James is a very selective person.
   ○ verb ○ noun ● adjective
3. The teacher selected three students to do problems on the board.
   ● verb ○ noun ○ adjective
4. Frank's selection of video games is enormous.
   ○ verb ● noun ○ adjective

Part 6

Underline the common part. Then combine the sentences with **and.**

1. Sal had nuts.
   Sal had bolts.
   Sal had nuts and bolts.
2. Joanna went to the park.
   Joanna picked four daisies.
   Joanna went to the park and picked four daisies.

☆Part 7

- A **compound word** is made by joining one word with another word.

  Example: rain + bow = rainbow

Write the compound word made by joining each pair of words.

1. bath + tub = bathtub
2. fire + place = fireplace
3. sun + set = sunset
4. sail + boat = sailboat
5. cat + fish = catfish
6. down + stairs = downstairs
7. birth + day = birthday
8. snow + ball = snowball

Part 1

Read the story and answer the questions.

> Terry got home from school and was excited about getting in his boat and sailing on the pond. However, when he got to the pond, he found it was completely frozen. Terry's brother, Wayne, was covering their boat with a tarp. "We can't sail until it warms up, Terry," Wayne said. "Boats won't float on ice. Of course, they won't sink, either, but we can't use our boat again until the spring."

1. Can the boat float on ice?   **No**
2. Can the boat sink in ice?   **No**
3. When can Terry sail again?
   In the spring.
4. Why was Wayne covering the boat with a tarp?   **They can't use their boat**
   until spring.
5. In what season do you think this happened?
   Winter

Part 2

Write **large intestine, esophagus, mouth, liver, stomach,** or **small intestine** in each blank.

1. **mouth**
2. **stomach**
3. **liver**
4. **small intestine**
5. **large intestine**
6. **esophagus**

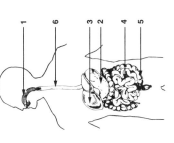
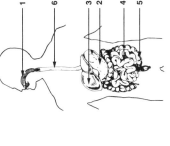

Deductions, graphic aids
Directions: If necessary, read the directions for each part. When students have completed the page, present each item and the answer. Correct any errors.

© 2001 SRA/McGraw-Hill. Permission is granted to reproduce for classroom use.

Part 3

Underline the common part. Then combine the sentences with **and**.

1. Omar liked to play football.
   Omar liked to read books.
   Omar liked to play football and
   read books.

2. The roller rink offered a deal.
   The roller rink had lots of customers.
   The roller rink offered a deal and
   had lots of customers.

3. Tanya made popcorn.
   Tanya rented a video.
   Tanya made popcorn and rented
   a video.

4. The dog ate the shoe.
   The dog buried the bone.
   The dog ate the shoe and buried
   the bone.

5. His dad bought two tomato cages.
   His dad bought a hoe.
   His dad bought two tomato cages
   and a hoe.

☆ Part 4

Write the **compound word** from the box below that best completes the sentence.

> newspaper   football   pancakes
> seashell   raincoat   classmate

1. Do I have time to read the **newspaper** ?
2. On Saturday we always have
   pancakes for breakfast.
3. Please wear your **raincoat** because it is raining.
4. My **classmate** let me borrow a piece of paper.
5. We found the prettiest **seashell** at the beach!

Part 5

Make each sentence begin with a capital letter. Put the correct punctuation mark at the end of each sentence.

1. W̲ where does this glass belong **?**
2. A̲ll that chalk is red **.**
3. H̲er friend stood over the crack **.**
4. W̲ho is going to be there **?**
5. C̲an you ride a bike **?**

Conjunctions, compound words, capitalization/punctuation
Directions: If necessary, read the directions for each part. When students have completed the page, present each item and the answer. Correct any errors.

46   © 2001 SRA/McGraw-Hill. Permission is granted to reproduce for classroom use.

LESSON 28   Name _____

Part 1

For each numbered word, write the letter of the word's definition.

1.	adjective	_e_	a. (n.) a word that tells the action that things do
2.	examine	_g_	b. (n.) a word that names a person, place, or thing
3.	large intestine	_j_	c. (n.) something that is selected
4.	liver	_h_	d. (n.) the organ that gives food to the blood
5.	noun	_b_	e. (n.) a word that comes before a noun and tells about the noun
6.	protect	_i_	f. (v.) choose
7.	select	_f_	g. (v.) look at
8.	selection	_c_	h. (n.) organ that makes chemicals that break down food
9.	small intestine	_d_	i. (v.) guard
10.	verb	_a_	j. (n.) the organ that stores food the body cannot use

LESSON 28   Name _____

Part 2

Read the story and answer the questions.

> Terry waited for spring. When it was nice and warm, he and Wayne went down to the pond. The ice had melted, so they uncovered their boat and pushed it into the water. As they were preparing to board their boat, it began to sink. Terry said, "Our boat's sinking!"
> Wayne said, "Well, that just proves that this is water. Boats sink in water, not in ice."

1. Why did Terry wait for spring to put the boat into the pond?
   So the pond wouldn't be frozen

2. What happened after Wayne and Terry pushed their boat into the water?
   It started to sink.

3. Would the boat have sunk in the ice?
   No

Part 3

Follow the directions.

1. Draw a square.

2. Draw a line from the lower left corner of the square to the upper right corner of the square.

3. Shade the area to the bottom right of the line.

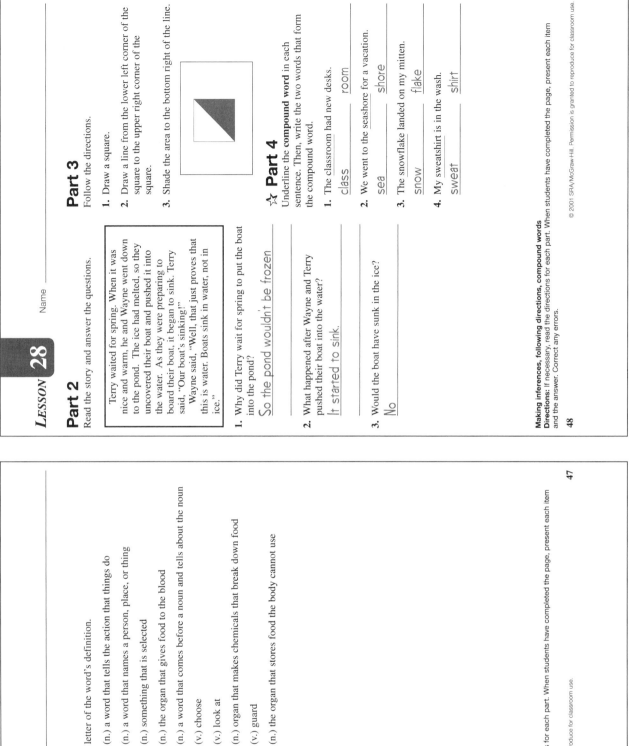

☆ Part 4

Underline the **compound word** in each sentence. Then, write the two words that form the compound word.

1. The classroom had new desks.
   class _____ room

2. We went to the seashore for a vacation.
   sea _____ shore

3. The snowflake landed on my mitten.
   snow _____ flake

4. My sweatshirt is in the wash.
   sweat _____ shirt

Part 1

Underline the common part. Then combine the sentences with **and.**

1. Coal is black.
   Ink is black.
   Coal and ink are black.

2. Two pans were on the stove.
   Two pots were on the stove.
   Two pots and two pans were on
   the stove.

3. Dogs eat meat.
   Lions eat meat.
   Dogs and lions eat meat.

4. Trey bumped his knee.
   Trey cut his finger.
   Trey bumped his knee and cut
   his finger.

5. A company constructed a building.
   A company constructed a dam.
   A company constructed a building
   and a dam.

6. Greg wanted to see the movie.
   Vicky wanted to see the movie.
   Greg and Vicky wanted to see
   the movie.

☆ Part 2

- Words that sound the same but are spelled differently are called **homophones.**
  Examples: sun/son so/sew blue/blew

Use the homophones in the box to complete the sentences below.

| sea | see | sail | sale | won | one |

1. The shoe __sale__ was last weekend.
2. I want to __sail__ to the island.
3. I can __see__ that you have not finished your dinner.
4. The __sea__ is calm this morning.
5. I __won__ a blue ribbon at the fair.
6. This is the __one__ I want to keep.

Part 3

Follow the directions.

1. Draw a big circle.
2. Draw a slanted line from the top left of the circle to the bottom right of the circle.
3. Draw a vertical line from the top of the circle to the center of the slanted line.
4. Shade in the smallest part.

Part 4

Fill in each blank.

1. mouth
2. large intestine
3. small intestine
4. esophagus
5. liver
6. stomach

Part 5

Use the rule to answer the questions.

The drier the air, the farther a baseball will travel.

1. Baseballs travel farther in summer air than in winter air.
   a. Which air is more humid?
      Winter
   b. How do you know?
      (Because baseballs
      travel farther in summer)

2. The air in Atlanta is more humid than the air in San Diego.
   a. In which city do baseballs travel farther?
      San Diego
   b. How do you know?
      (Because the air in
      Atlanta is more humid)

137

LESSON 30 Name _____

☆ Part 1
Use the **homophones** in the box to complete the sentences below.

| here hear write right ate eight |
| for four way weigh new knew |

Use the homophones in the box to complete the sentences below.

1. Did you __hear__ the fire alarm?
2. Please put your library book __here__.
3. I think I __knew__ the answer.
4. Our __new__ car is a station wagon.
5. Please wait __for__ me.
6. Did she have __four__ sisters?
7. I __write__ with my left hand.
8. Turn __right__ at the stop sign.
9. I will __weigh__ the potatoes.
10. Did you say to go this __way__?
11. I __ate__ a piece of toast for breakfast.
12. There are __eight__ boys in our class.

Part 2
Complete the instructions.

1. Draw two __horizontal__ lines.
2. Write the word __pelvis__ at the __left__ end of the lower line.
3. Write the word __femur__ below the __right__ end of the lower line.

Homophones, following directions
Directions: If necessary, read the directions for each part. When students have completed the page, present each item and the answer. Correct any errors.

LESSON 30 Name _____

Part 3
Fill in each blank with the word that has the same meaning as the word or words below the blank.

1. Many monkeys __examine__ (look at) each other for ticks and mites.
2. The director __selected__ (chose) an actor for her play.
3. That boy is __constructing__ (building) a soapbox racer.
4. Luke __obtained__ (got) the video game he wanted.

Part 4
Complete the analogies.

1. Tell what class each thing is in.
   A **car** is to __vehicles__ as a **box** is to __containers__.
2. Tell what each thing is made of.
   A **car** is to __metal__ as a **box** is to __cardboard__.
3. Tell what each thing is made to do.
   A **car** is to __taking people places__ as a **box** is to __putting things in__.

Part 5
Use the rule to answer the questions.

| **If you don't get enough iron in your diet, you can get tired easily.** |

1. Bailey doesn't get enough iron in his diet.
   a. What happens to Bailey?
   __He gets tired easily.__
   b. How do you know?
   __(Because he doesn't get enough iron)__
2. Peg never gets tired.
   a. What do you know about Peg?
   __She gets enough iron.__
   b. How do you know?
   __(Because she never gets tired)__
3. Mark takes vitamins that contain iron. Frank never takes any vitamins.
   a. Which person is more likely to get tired?
   __Frank__
   b. How do you know?
   __(Because he never takes vitamins that contain iron)__

Vocabulary, analogies, making inferences
Directions: If necessary, read the directions for each part. When students have completed the page, present each item and the answer. Correct any errors.

☆ Part 1

Read each sentence. Draw a line through the **homophone** that is used incorrectly. Then write the correct word in the blank.

1. We went in the ~~knew~~ car. new _____

2. I have ~~for~~ dollars in my pocket.
   four _____

3. We ~~eight~~ dinner at six o'clock. ate _____

4. The wind ~~blue~~ my hat off. blew _____

5. I want to get the ~~write~~ answer. right _____

6. We were all ~~scent~~ home. sent _____

7. The coat ~~sail~~ was in August. sale _____

8. I like to wear my ~~hare~~ in pigtails.
   hair _____

Part 2

Fill in each blank.

1. small intestine

2. mouth

3. stomach

4. large intestine

5. liver

6. esophagus

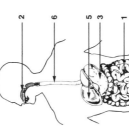

Homophones, graphic aids
Directions: If necessary, read the directions for each part. When students have completed the page, present each item and the answer. Correct any errors.

Part 3

Underline the nouns. Draw a line over the adjectives. Circle the verbs.

1. My friend (constructs) rocking horses.

2. Those men (are constructing) houses.

3. Boys and girls (watched) the construction.

4. His friends (play) near the construction.

5. Builders (constructed) that church.

Part 4

Complete the instructions.

1. Draw a _____ horizontal _____ line.

2. Draw a _____ circle _____ above the
   _____ horizontal _____ line.

3. Write the word _____ protect _____ under the
   _____ horizontal _____ line.

Part 5

Use the rule to answer the questions.

> You get a disease called scurvy if you don't get any vitamin C.

1. Janice doesn't get any vitamin C.
   a. What will happen to Janice?
      Janice will get scurvy.

   b. How do you know?
      (Because she doesn't get any
      vitamin C)

2. Chris got scurvy.
   a. What else do you know about Chris?
      Chris didn't get any vitamin C.

   b. How do you know?
      (Because he got scurvy)

3. Matt eats oranges, which have lots of vitamin C. Francis never eats oranges or any other foods with vitamin C.
   a. Which person well get scurvy?
      Francis

   b. How do you know?
      (Because he never eats food
      with vitamin C)

Conventions of grammar, following directions, making inferences
Directions: If necessary, read the directions for each part. When students have completed the page, present each item and the answer. Correct any errors.

140

Part 1

Write a word that comes from **obtain** or **construct** in each blank. Fill in the correct circle next to **verb**, **noun**, or **adjective**.

1. A carpenter is ___constructing___ a ship with a hammer.
   ● verb ○ noun ○ adjective

2. The ___construction___ of that road will take eight years.
   ○ verb ● noun ○ adjective

3. Lori will ___obtain___ several dogs from the pound.
   ● verb ○ noun ○ adjective

☆ Part 2

> • An **adjective** is a word that describes a noun. It tells *which one, how many,* or *what kind.*
> Example: **The two** dogs made **a loud** noise.

Underline the adjectives.

1. The big deer ran back into the woods.
2. Martin ate two bites of his sandwich.
3. The noisy car stopped at the corner.
4. My older sister wanted to go to the prom.
5. We walked inside the new house.
6. Dancing is good exercise.
7. Jenny asked for five dollars for the mall.
8. Isn't the new grocery store open?
9. Chocolate milkshakes are my favorite.
10. Your new puppy likes to eat socks.

Part 3

Fill in each blank.

1. ___stomach___
2. ___liver___
3. ___large intestine___
4. ___mouth___
5. ___small intestine___
6. ___esophagus___

Part 4

Underline the common part. Then combine the sentences with **and.**

1. Asa cleans the house for fun.
   Rachel cleans the house for fun.
   <u>Asa and Rachel clean the house for fun.</u>

2. A dolphin swims in the ocean.
   A marlin swims in the ocean.
   <u>A dolphin and a marlin swim in the ocean.</u>

3. Nick obtained oil.
   Nick oiled his bike chain.
   <u>Nick obtained oil and oiled his bike chain.</u>

4. This rabbit burrows in cedar chips.
   That rabbit burrows in cedar chips.
   <u>This rabbit and that rabbit burrow in cedar chips.</u>

5. Carly grows beans.
   Carly kills weeds.
   <u>Carly grows beans and kills weeds.</u>

Part 1

Write **quadriceps, biceps,** or **abdominal muscle** in each blank.

1. quadriceps
2. abdominal muscle
3. biceps

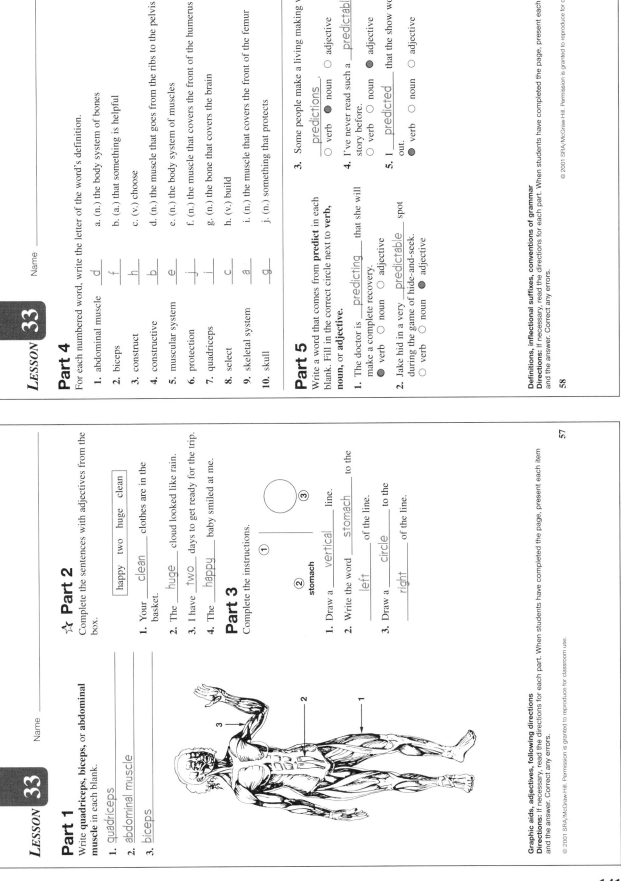

☆ Part 2

Complete the sentences with adjectives from the box.

| happy   two   huge   clean |

1. Your __clean__ clothes are in the basket.
2. The __huge__ cloud looked like rain.
3. I have __two__ days to get ready for the trip.
4. The __happy__ baby smiled at me.

Part 3

Complete the instructions.

1. Draw a __vertical__ line.
2. Write the word __stomach__ to the left of the line.
3. Draw a __circle__ to the right of the line.

Graphic aids, adjectives, following directions
Directions: If necessary, read the directions for each part. When students have completed the page, present each item and the answer. Correct any errors.

© 2001 SRA/McGraw-Hill. Permission is granted to reproduce for classroom use.

57

Part 4

For each numbered word, write the letter of the word's definition.

1. abdominal muscle __d__
2. biceps __f__
3. construct __h__
4. constructive __b__
5. muscular system __e__
6. protection __j__
7. quadriceps __i__
8. select __c__
9. skeletal system __a__
10. skull __g__

a. (n.) the body system of bones
b. (a.) that something is helpful
c. (v.) choose
d. (n.) the muscle that goes from the ribs to the pelvis
e. (n.) the body system of muscles
f. (n.) the muscle that covers the front of the humerus
g. (n.) the bone that covers the brain
h. (v.) build
i. (n.) the muscle that covers the front of the femur
j. (n.) something that protects

Part 5

Write a word that comes from **predict** in each blank. Fill in the correct circle next to **verb, noun,** or **adjective.**

1. The doctor is __predicting__ that she will make a complete recovery.
   ● verb ○ noun ○ adjective
2. Jake hid in a very __predictable__ spot during the game of hide-and-seek.
   ○ verb ○ noun ● adjective
3. Some people make a living making weather __predictions__.
   ○ verb ● noun ○ adjective
4. I've never read such a __predictable__ story before.
   ○ verb ○ noun ● adjective
5. I __predicted__ that the show would sell out.
   ● verb ○ noun ○ adjective

Definitions, inflectional suffixes, conventions of grammar
Directions: If necessary, read the directions for each part. When students have completed the page, present each item and the answer. Correct any errors.

58

© 2001 SRA/McGraw-Hill. Permission is granted to reproduce for classroom use.

141

142

Part 1

Complete the instructions.

femur
① ____
② △
③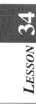

1. Draw a ___slanted___ line down to the right.

2. Draw a ___triangle___ above the right end of the line.

3. Write the word ___femur___ below the ___left___ end of the line.

Part 2

Read the story and answer the questions.

> Terry and Wayne began building a new boat to sail on the pond. They searched around and found some lumber in a garbage pile. Terry said, "I want to make this boat even bigger than the last one."
> Wayne shook his head at his brother and said, "Terry, we don't have enough wood to make this boat as big as the one that sank. Either we'll have to wait to get more wood, or we'll have to make this boat smaller than the one that sank."

1. What does Terry want to do?
   ___Make this boat bigger than the___
   ___last one___

2. Why can't they make a boat that's bigger than the one that sank?
   ___(Because they don't have___
   ___enough wood)___

3. If they don't get more lumber, the boat they build will have to be ___smaller.___

4. What do the boys need to build a bigger boat?
   ___More wood___

Following directions, making inferences
Directions: If necessary, read the directions for each part. When students have completed the page, present each item and the answer. Correct any errors.

Part 3

Write **biceps**, **abdominal muscle**, or **quadriceps** in each blank.

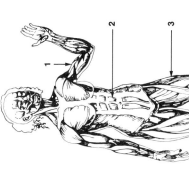

1. ___biceps___

2. ___abdominal muscle___

3. ___quadriceps___

☆ Part 4

Read each sentence. Underline each **adjective**. Circle the person, place, or thing the adjective describes.

1. He liked the brown (jacket).

2. I wanted raisin (bread) for breakfast.

3. Sherry ate three (bananas) today.

4. The white (snow) looked pretty.

5. I wished for a baby (brother) on my (birthday).

6. The old (lighthouse) was close to the (ocean).

7. My favorite (aunt) was coming for a (visit).

8. Three (weeks) have passed since we had rain.

Graphic aids, adjectives
Directions: If necessary, read the directions for each part. When students have completed the page, present each item and the answer. Correct any errors.

Part 1

Write the number of the fact that explains why each thing happened.

1. Cows give milk.
2. Cows eat grass.

__2__ a. The man who owned the cow never cut his grass.

____ b. The man made butter at home.

____ c. The cow ate green things.

__2__ d. The man did not buy milk at the store.

Part 2

Write a word that comes from **select** or **predict** in each blank. Fill in the correct circle next to **verb, noun,** or **adjective.**

1. My video store has a wide __selection__ of movies to rent.
   ○ verb ● noun ○ adjective

2. I don't like movies with __predictable__ endings.
   ○ verb ○ noun ● adjective

3. I can __select__ any type of movie I want to see at my video store.
   ● verb ○ noun ○ adjective

Part 3

Write **abdominal muscle, quadriceps,** or **biceps** in each blank.

1. __biceps__
2. __quadriceps__
3. __abdominal muscle__

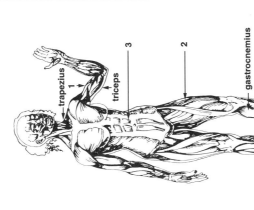

trapezius

triceps — 1

3

2

gastrocnemius

Drawing conclusions based on evidence, inflectional suffixes/conventions of grammar, graphic aids
Directions: If necessary, read the directions for each part. When students have completed the page, present each item and the answer. Correct any errors.

☆ Part 4

• An **adverb** is a word that describes a verb. It tells *how, when,* or *where.* Many adverbs end in **–ly.**
  Examples:
  The horse walked **slowly. How?**
  The horse walked **today. When?**
  The horse walked **here. Where?**

Underline each adverb. Then write **how, when,** or **where** on the lines provided.

1. Tom eats dinner late. __when__

2. Amy ran quickly. __how__

3. The cat sat there. __where__

Complete each sentence with an adverb from the box below. Choose an adverb that answers the question in ( ).

| slowly | early | near |

4. I live __near__ the school. (Where?)

5. Grandma walked up the stairs __slowly__. (How?)

6. Dad left for work __early__. (When?)

Part 5

Complete the analogy.

Prediction is to noun

1. as **protect** is to __verb__.

2. as **selective** is to __adjective__.

3. as **construction** is to __noun__.

Part 6

Underline the common part. Then combine the sentences with **and.**

1. The woman was mad.
   Her husband was mad.
   __The woman and her husband__
   __were mad.__

2. Monkeys were climbing in trees.
   Monkeys were searching for nuts.
   __Monkeys were climbing in trees__
   __and searching for nuts.__

3. Clem was reading in the library.
   Stan was reading in the library.
   __Clem and Sam were reading in__
   __the library.__

Adverbs, analogies, conjunctions
Directions: If necessary, read the directions for each part. When students have completed the page, present each item and the answer. Correct any errors.

LESSON 36

Name _____

Part 1

Underline each contradiction.

1. All dogs have four legs.

a. All dogs have three legs.

b. No dogs have four legs.

c. Only some dogs have four legs.

d. Every dog has four legs.

2. Jill is bigger than Carol.

a. Jill is not bigger than Carol.

b. Carol is smaller than Jill.

c. Jill is smaller than Carol.

d. Carol is not as big as Jill.

Part 2

Complete the instructions.

① ▽

② ◁

③ —

1. Draw a ___triangle___ pointing ___down___.

2. Draw a ___triangle___ pointing ___up___, under the other triangle.

3. Draw a ___horizontal___ line underneath the ___triangle___ pointing ___up___.

Contradictions, following directions, adverbs
Directions: If necessary, read the directions for each part. When students have completed the page, present each item and the answer. Correct any errors.

LESSON 36

Name _____

Part 3

☆ Underline the **adverb** in each sentence. What question does the adverb answer? Write the answer on the line.

1. I walked quickly down the street.
   How? Quickly

2. She will return soon.
   When? Soon

3. David lives across the street.
   Where? Across

4. I will eat lunch early today.
   When? Early

5. The clouds are above our heads.
   Where? Above

6. The lions roared loudly.
   How? Loudly

7. The children walked slowly into the assembly.
   How? Slowly

8. The sun shines brightly.
   How? Brightly

Part 4

Write **trapezius**, **triceps**, or **gastrocnemius** in each blank.

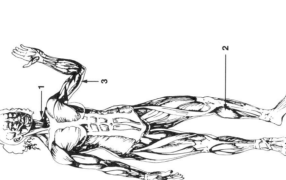

1. trapezius

2. gastrocnemius

3. triceps

Part 5

Read the story and answer the questions. Circle the **W** if the question is answered by words in the story, and underline those words. Circle the **D** if the question is answered by a deduction.

> Kyle did not know which park to play at. He said to himself, " My sister is swimming at the Aqua Park, but my brother is playing kickball at the Athletic Field. I like both of those activities, but I think I'll go to the Aqua Park and swim, because that place will stay cooler when it gets hot this afternoon." So Kyle went to the Aqua Park.

1. Where was Kyle's brother playing kickball? **W** Ⓓ
   At the Athletic Field

2. Which activity did Kyle prefer? **W** Ⓓ
   Neither

3. Why did Kyle choose the Aqua Park over the Athletic Field? **W** Ⓓ
   (Because it would stay cooler)

4. Did Kyle like it better when it was hotter or cooler? **W** Ⓓ
   Cooler

Graphic aids, deductions
Directions: If necessary, read the directions for each part. When students have completed the page, present each item and the answer. Correct any errors.

☆ Part 1

The words in the box below are **adverbs**. Write each word under a heading to show if the word tells **how, when,** or **where.**

late	soon	brightly	early
loudly	yesterday	near	there
fast	here	away	slowly

How?	**When?**	**Where?**
loudly	late	here
fast	soon	near
brightly	yesterday	away
slowly	early	there

Part 2

Complete the instructions.

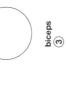
① (circle)

② skeletal

③ biceps

1. Draw a ____circle____ .

2. Write the word ____skeletal____ to the left of the ____circle____ .

3. Write the word **biceps** ____below____ the ____circle____ .

Part 3

Underline each contradiction.

The small intestine is in the digestive system.

a. The small intestine is a bone.

b. The small intestine protects body parts.

c. The small intestine is in the skeletal system.

d. The small intestine is in the system of muscles.

Part 4

Write **trapezius, quadriceps, gastrocnemius, biceps, abdominal muscle,** or **triceps** in each blank.

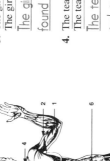

1. triceps

2. biceps

3. gastrocnemius

4. trapezius

5. quadriceps

6. abdominal muscle

Part 5

Underline the common part. Then combine the sentences with **and.**

1. Joey was playing basketball.
Tom was playing basketball.
Joey and Tom were
playing basketball.

2. Andre ran on the track.
Andre listened to his radio.
Andre ran on the track and listened
to his radio.

3. The girls followed the creek.
The girls found a field.
The girls followed the creek and
found a field.

4. The teacher gave Will a detention.
The teacher gave Will extra homework.
The teacher gave Will a detention
and extra homework.

5. My brother was falling asleep.
Dad was falling asleep.
My brother and Dad were
falling asleep.

LESSON 38

Name _____

Part 1

For each numbered word, write the letter of the word's definition.

a. (n.) the muscle that covers the back of the humerus
b. (n.) the muscle that covers the back of the neck
c. (v.) build
d. (n.) something that is selected
e. (n.) the bones that cover the organs in the chest
f. (n.) a statement that predicts
g. (n.) the backbone
h. (n.) the muscle that covers the back of the lower leg

1. prediction _f_
2. triceps _a_
3. gastrocnemius _h_
4. construct _c_
5. selection _d_
6. trapezius _b_
7. spine _g_
8. ribs _e_

Part 2

Underline each contradiction.

| The triceps is a muscle. |

a. The triceps is in the muscular system.
b. The triceps is not in the skeletal system.
c. The triceps is a bone.
d. The triceps is part of the digestive system.

LESSON 38

Name _____

Part 3

Complete the instructions.

examination
③

① ◯
obtained
②

1. Draw a ____circle____.
2. Write the word **obtained** ____above____ the ____circle____.
3. Write the word **examination** ____below____ the ____circle____.

☆ Part 4

Use a **comma** (,) after the words **yes** and **no** if they begin a sentence.
Example: Yes, you may go now.

Use a **comma** to separate three or more items listed together in a sentence.
Example: I had juice, cereal, toast, and eggs for breakfast.

Read the sentences below. Add commas where they are needed.

1. No, the band was not in the parade.
2. Horses, cows, pigs, and goats live in the country.
3. Yes, I was sick yesterday.

Part 5

Write a word that comes from **reside** in each blank. Fill in the correct circle next to **verb, noun,** or **adjective.**

1. They don't allow warehouses in ____residential____ areas.
   ○ verb ○ noun ● adjective

2. Some people do not have permanent ____residences____.
   ○ verb ● noun ○ adjective

3. Many ducks ____reside____ near water.
   ● verb ○ noun ○ adjective

4. An apartment is usually a cheaper ____residence____ than a house.
   ○ verb ● noun ○ adjective

5. Firefighters actually ____reside____ at the firehouse.
   ● verb ○ noun ○ adjective

Part 1

Write **abdominal muscle, triceps, biceps, trapezius, gastrocnemius,** or **quadriceps** for each blank.

1. quadriceps
2. gastrocnemius
3. abdominal muscle
4. trapezius
5. biceps
6. triceps

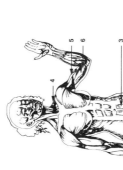

☆ Part 2

Read each sentence. Then place commas where they are needed in each sentence.

1. I sleep with a sheet, a blanket, and a bedspread to keep warm.

2. John's favorite foods are pizza, peaches, and corn.

3. Larry has lived in Ohio, Kentucky, and New Jersey.

4. Remember to pack the chairs, cooler, beach towels, lotion, and toys for the beach.

5. Terry's favorite subjects are math, science, and art.

6. Sandy has a dog, a cat, a rabbit, and a hamster as pets.

7. Please make your bed, brush your teeth, walk the dog, and put out the trash.

8. Let's go to the beach, the museum, and the zoo on our trip.

Part 3

Underline the common part. Then combine the sentences with **and.**

1. Kate was protecting the candy.
   Ann was protecting the candy.
   Kate and Ann were protecting the candy.

2. Maury likes oranges.
   Cynthia likes oranges.
   Maury and Cynthia like oranges.

3. Steve speaks English.
   Steve speaks Spanish.
   Steve speaks English and Spanish.

4. Table tennis was fun to play.
   Pool was fun to play.
   Table tennis and pool were fun to play.

5. Poodles are smart.
   Poodles are peppy.
   Poodles are smart and peppy.

Part 4

Cross out the words that are in the rule and the conclusion. Then write the middle part.

1. Every noun names a person, place, or thing.
   Lawrence is a noun.

   So, **Lawrence** names a person, place, or thing.

2. Some dogs have straight hair.
   A terrier is a dog.

   So, maybe a terrier has straight hair.

3. The woman found some bones.
   A humerus is a bone.

   So, maybe the woman found a humerus.

147

Part 1

Make each contradiction true.

> **Steve is shorter than Jim.**

shorter

1. Steve is ~~not~~ *taller* than Jim.
2. Steve is ~~not~~ *taller* than Jim.
3. Jim is shorter than Steve.
4. Jim is not shorter than Steve.

Part 2

Complete the instructions.

① ② ③ **triceps**

1. Draw a ___horizontal___ line.
2. Draw a vertical line ___down___ from the ___right___ end of the horizontal line.
3. Write the word ___triceps___ ___to the left___ of the ___vertical___ line.

☆ Part 3

Look at each pair of sentences. Underline the sentence in which the **commas** are correctly placed.

1. Please put away your books, pencils, and paper.

   Please put away your books pencils, and paper.

2. Bill, Jane Tracy and Brad all ride the same bus.

   Bill, Jane, Tracy, and Brad all ride the same bus.

3. I like to ride bikes, play video games and skateboard.

   I like to ride bikes, play video games, and skateboard.

4. My favorite fruits are oranges, peaches, grapes, and watermelon.

   My favorite fruits are oranges, peaches, grapes and watermelon.

5. Monday, and Wednesday I work out.

   Monday and Wednesday I work out.

Contractions, following directions, commas
Directions: If necessary, read the directions for each part. When students have completed the page, present each item and the answer. Correct any errors.

© 2001 SRA/McGraw-Hill. Permission is granted to reproduce for classroom use.

71

Part 4

Write the conclusion of each deduction.

1. Everything you drink goes down your esophagus.
   Water is something you drink.
   So, water goes down your esophagus.

2. Some bones are joined to two other bones.
   The tibia is a bone.
   So, maybe the tibia is joined to two other bones.

3. Jack has some dogs.
   A Scottish terrier is a dog.
   So, maybe Jack has a Scottish terrier.

Part 5

Underline the common part. Then combine the sentences with **and.**

1. Katie is reading a book.
   Sam is reading a book.
   Katie and Sam are reading a book.

2. Six ducks were flying.
   A robin was flying.
   Six ducks and a robin were flying.

3. This dog is friendly.
   That cat is friendly.
   This dog and that cat are friendly.

4. Sally has a headache.
   Sally has a toothache.
   Sally has a headache and a toothache.

Deductions, conjunctions/writing
Directions: If necessary, read the directions for each part. When students have completed the page, present each item and the answer. Correct any errors.

72   © 2001 SRA/McGraw-Hill. Permission is granted to reproduce for classroom use.

148

LESSON 41

Name _____

Part 1

Make each contradiction true.

The biceps is in the muscular system.

1. The biceps is a bone.
   muscle
2. The biceps is in the system of bones.
   muscles
3. The biceps is in the ~~digestive~~ system.
   muscular
4. A two-headed ~~muscle~~ is in the ~~skeletal~~
   muscular   muscular
   system.

Part 2

Cross out the words that are in the rule and the conclusion. Then write the middle part.

1. Most women have hair on their head.
   Carol is a woman.

   So, maybe Carol has hair on her head.

   Carol is a woman.

2. A muscle does not move the bone it covers.
   A triceps is a muscle.

   So, a triceps does not move the bone it covers.

   A triceps is a muscle.

3. Some nouns come from verbs.
   House is a noun.

   So, maybe **house** comes from a verb.

   House is a noun.

Part 3

Fill in each blank.

1. quadriceps
2. abdominal muscle
3. gastrocnemius
4. biceps
5. triceps
6. trapezius

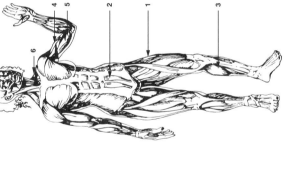

Contradictions, writing deductions, graphic aids
Directions: If necessary, read the directions for each part. When students have completed the page, present each item and the answer. Correct any errors

© 2001 SRA/McGraw-Hill. Permission is granted to reproduce for classroom use.

73

LESSON 41

Name _____

☆ Part 4

Use a **capital letter** to begin most **abbreviations.**
Use a **period** at the end of an **abbreviation.**
Doctor Boyle **Dr.** Boyle
Mister Carver **Mr.** Carver

Write the names. Use capital letters and periods where they are needed.

mrs crotty	Mrs. Crotty
dr thompson	Dr. Thompson
mr lyons	Mr. Lyons
mrs brown	Mrs. Brown
mr lewis	Mr. Lewis
mrs berry	Mrs. Berry
dr timko	Dr. Timko
mr wilt	Mr. Wilt
dr zimmerman	Dr. Zimmerman
ms alcorn	Ms. Alcorn

Part 5

Fill in each blank with the word that has the same meaning as the word or words under the blank.

| constructed | protect |
| reside | predict |

1. Firefighters ___predict___
   (say it will happen)
   that smoke alarms will save lives.

2. Many bats ___reside___ in caves.
   (live)

3. Brushing your teeth will ___protect___
   them from decay.   (guard)

4. The stairs are ___constructed___ of wood.
   (built)

Abbreviations, vocabulary
Directions: If necessary, read the directions for each part. When students have completed the page, present each item and the answer. Correct any errors.

74

© 2001 SRA/McGraw-Hill. Permission is granted to reproduce for classroom use.

149

150

Part 1

Follow the directions.

1. Draw a line that slants down to the left.

2. Write the word **liver** at the top end of the line.

3. Write the word **mouth** at the bottom end of the line.

liver

mouth

Part 2

Underline the common part. Then combine the sentences with **and.**

1. Joey likes to predict the weather.
   Tamara likes to predict the weather.
   Joey and Tamara like to predict the weather.

2. That dog has floppy ears.
   That dog has a long tail.
   That dog has floppy ears and a long tail.

3. Tony has a green shirt.
   Tony has blue pants.
   Tony has a green shirt and blue pants.

☆ Part 3

An initial is the first letter of a name. Capitalize an initial and put a period after it.
Example: **M. C. Wells** for **Mary Coe Wells**

Write the names. Use capital letters and periods where they are needed.

1. a c kenny — A. C. Kenny
2. mrs m l lewis — Mrs. M. L. Lewis
3. mr r d willams — Mr. R. D. Williams
4. a a milne — A. A. Milne
5. mrs p overman — Mrs. P. Overman
6. e b white — E. B. White
7. ms bacall — Ms. Bacall
8. r c ward — R. C. Ward

Part 4

Read the story and answer the questions. Circle the **W** if the question is answered by words in the story, and underline those words. Circle the **D** if the question is answered by a deduction.

After looking around for a month, Terry and Wayne had obtained enough wood to make a bigger boat than the one that sank. They worked for a week constructing the new boat. When it was finished, Terry wanted to launch it into the pond immediately. "Wait a second," Wayne said. "It's bad luck to launch a boat before naming it. We need a good name for it."

Terry thought for a moment. "I know, why not *The Twayne?*" Wayne agreed and smiled.

1. Why did the boat need a name before Terry and Wayne launched it into the pond?
   (Because it's bad luck to launch a boat before naming it)   **W** D

2. How did Terry come up with the name "The Twayne" for the boat?
   (He combined "Terry" and "Wayne.")   W **D**

Part 5

Make each contradiction true.

All cats have a spine.

1. That kitten has a spine.
2. Her cat has ~~no~~ a backbone.
3. ~~Only~~ All some cats have a spine.
4. ~~A few~~ All cats have a backbone.

Part 1

For each numbered word, write the letter of the word's definition.

a. (v.) look at
b. (v.) live somewhere
c. (a.) that a place has many residences
d. (n.) the hip bone
e. (n.) the upper arm bone
f. (n.) a place where someone resides
g. (v.) say that something will happen
h. (a.) that something protects
i. (n.) the upper leg bone
j. (a.) that something is easy to predict

1. residence ___f___
2. predictable ___j___
3. humerus ___e___
4. examine ___a___
5. residential ___c___
6. pelvis ___d___
7. reside ___b___
8. femur ___i___
9. protective ___h___
10. predict ___g___

Part 2

Write the number of the fact that explains why each thing happened.

1. Keri is building up her biceps.
2. Alice broke her femur.

a. She has a cast on her leg. ___2___
b. She swims every other day. ___1___
c. She lifts weights. ___1___
d. She was in the hospital overnight. ___2___

Definitions, drawing conclusions based on evidence
Directions: If necessary, read the directions for each part. When students have completed the page, present each item and the answer. Correct any errors.
© 2001 SRA/McGraw-Hill. Permission is granted to reproduce for classroom use.
77

☆ Part 3

Use a capital letter to begin an abbreviation for the name of a place.
Example:
Road: Rd.   Street: St.   Drive: Dr.
Avenue: Ave.   Court: Ct.

Write the name using the correct abbreviation. Use capital letters and periods where needed.

1. maple street
   Maple St.

2. princeton road
   Princeton Rd.

3. boston avenue
   Boston Ave.

4. franklin road
   Franklin Rd.

5. forest highlands court
   Forest Highlands Ct.

6. riverside drive
   Riverside Dr.

Part 4

Make each contradiction true.

Tia never selected a book with a
predictable ending.

1. The book that Tia selected ~~had~~ a predictable didn't have
   ending.
   always
2. Tia ~~never~~ chose a book with a surprise
   ending.

3. Tia never selected a book that had an ending
   that could be predicted.

Abbreviations, contradictions
Directions: If necessary, read the directions for each part. When students have completed the page, present each item and the answer. Correct any errors.
78
© 2001 SRA/McGraw-Hill. Permission is granted to reproduce for classroom use.

LESSON 44 — Name ____

Part 1

Underline the nouns. Draw a line over the adjectives. Circle the verbs.

1. Squirrels are foraging near that stream.
2. Dust swirled in the bright sunlight.
3. The playful puppies attacked his socks.
4. The beans filled the jar.
5. My computer uses a color monitor.

Part 2

Complete the instructions.

③ skeletal

① /

muscular
②

1. Draw a line that slants down to the right _____ .

2. Write the word __muscular__ __below__ the line.

3. Write the word __skeletal__ __above__ the line.

☆ Part 3

> A **pronoun** is a part of speech. It takes the place of a noun. Some pronouns are **he, she, it, we, you, they,** and **I.**
> **Example:** Will plays with Brian. He plays with Brian.

Rewrite these sentences. Choose a pronoun from the box below to take the place of the underlined word or words.

He   She   We   They

1. Leslie got a gift.
   (He/She) got a gift.

2. James went to the baseball game.
   He went to the baseball game.

3. Wendy and Chris are going shopping.
   (They are going shopping.)
   (We are going shopping.)

4. Suzi and I like to travel together.
   (We like to travel together.)
   (They like to travel together.)

LESSON 44 — Name ____

Part 4

Fill in the circle next to **one** or **more than one** after each sentence. Write **were** or **was** in each blank.

1. The boy __was__ sad.
   ● one   ○ more than one

2. His brother __was__ sad.
   ● one   ○ more than one

3. The boys __were__ sad.
   ○ one   ● more than one

4. Those girls and that boy __were__ sad.
   ○ one   ● more than one

Part 5

Make each contradiction true.

> That dog always protects this yard.

1. This yard is always protected by that dog.
   ~~always~~

2. This yard is ~~never~~ guarded by that dog.
   always

3. The dog ~~never~~ gives this yard protection.
   always

4. That dog ~~sometimes~~ protects this yard.

Part 6

Fill in each blank.

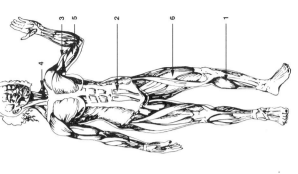

1. __gastrocnemius__
2. __abdominal muscle__
3. __biceps__
4. __trapezius__
5. __triceps__
6. __quadriceps__

152

Part 1

Fill in each blank.

1. mouth
2. liver
3. small intestine
4. large intestine
5. stomach
6. esophagus

Part 2

Make each contradiction true.

> **Only an adjective describes a person, place, or thing.**

1. ~~Some~~ No verbs describe a place.
2. **Dog** is ∧not an adjective.
3. **Beautiful** can describe a person, place, or thing.
4. **Chicago** names a place.

Part 3

Write the number of the fact that explains why each thing happened.

1. Sam is protective of his CDs.
2. Scott makes predictions about movie endings.

a. He uses cleaner on his collection.   1
b. He says how the movie will end.   2
c. He keeps his CDs in their cases.   1
d. He says that things will happen.   2

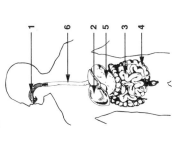
1 6 2 5 3 4

Graphic aids, contradictions, drawing conclusions based on evidence
Directions: If necessary, read the directions for each part. When students have completed the page, present each item and the answer. Correct any errors.
© 2001 SRA/McGraw-Hill. Permission is granted to reproduce for classroom use.

☆ Part 4

Circle the pronouns in each sentence.

1. (We) visited the Statue of Liberty.
2. The ranger gave (us) a tour.
3. (He) showed (us) the movie.
4. (We) went to Ellis Island, too.
5. (I) liked (it) the best!
6. Maybe (we) can go back next year.
7. (It) took a long time to get home.
8. (We) all slept well that night.

Part 5

Write what each analogy tells.

- What part of speech each word is
- What verb each word comes from
- What each word means
- What ending each word has

1. **Construction** is to **noun** as **protection** is to **noun.**
   What part of speech each word is

2. **Residence** is to **ence** as **protection** is to **ion.**
   What ending each word has

3. **Construction** is to **construct** as **residence** is to **reside.**
   What verb each word comes from

Pronouns, analogies
Directions: If necessary, read the directions for each part. When students have completed the page, present each item and the answer. Correct any errors.
© 2001 SRA/McGraw-Hill. Permission is granted to reproduce for classroom use.

LESSON 46 Name _____

☆ Part 1

Read each sentence. Write the pronoun that best fits the meaning.

1. The dog played with the bone and then buried ___it___.
2. Jason said, "Please give the paper to ___me___."
3. The boy said ___he___ heard a loud noise.
4. Gretchen lost ___her___ glove.
5. The family ate and discussed ___their___ plans for the day.
6. Mike asked if we could meet ___him___.
7. Will Gary and Lyn fly when ___they___ go to Florida?
8. Sally said ___her___ cold was getting better.

Part 2

Underline the common part. Then combine the sentences with **and**.

1. Joe ate his cereal.
   Joe ate his toast.
   Joe ate his cereal and toast.

2. Amy selected a book.
   Amy selected a CD.
   Amy selected a book and a CD.

3. Vince shot several jump shots.
   Vince shot several free throws.
   Vince shot several jump shots and free throws.

4. Nigel ran with his dog.
   Nigel ran with Liane.
   Nigel ran with his dog and Liane.

5. Homer is very funny.
   Homer is very wise.
   Homer is very funny and wise.

Pronouns, conjunctions/writing sentences
Directions: If necessary, read the directions for each part. When students have completed the page, present each item and the answer. Correct any errors.

© 2001 SRA/McGraw-Hill. Permission is granted to reproduce for classroom use.

83

LESSON 46 Name _____

Part 3

Write what each analogy tells.

- What body system each thing is in
- How many parts
- What bone each thing covers

1. **Quadriceps** is to **femur** as **triceps** is to **humerus.**
   What bone each thing covers

2. **Quadriceps** is to the **muscular system** as **biceps** is to the **muscular system.**
   What body system each thing is in

3. **Quadriceps** is to **four** as **biceps** is to **two.**
   How many parts

Part 4

Cross out the words that are in the rule and the conclusion. Then write the middle part.

1. Lonnie has some cats.
   A Siamese is a cat.
   So, maybe Lonnie has a Siamese.

2. Some words are not nouns.
   Silly is a word.
   So, maybe **silly** is not a noun.

3. Every muscle does a job.
   The triceps is a muscle.
   So, the triceps does a job.

Part 5

Follow the directions.

1. Draw a horizontal line.
2. Draw a vertical line down from the center of the horizontal line.
3. Write the word skeletal at the bottom of the vertical line.

skeletal

Analogies/writing analogies, following directions
Directions: If necessary, read the directions for each part. When students have completed the page, present each item and the answer. Correct any errors.

84

© 2001 SRA/McGraw-Hill. Permission is granted to reproduce for classroom use.

Part 1

Write **who** or **which** after each item.

1. Four women — who
2. His dad — who
3. His hat — which
4. Our teacher — who
5. Two spoons — which
6. Her liver — which
7. A young woman — who
8. His skin — which
9. Those cows — which
10. An orange — which

Part 2

Make each statement mean the same thing as the statement in the box.

> The trainer examined **Cory's quadriceps.**

1. The trainer looked at Cory's ~~three-headed~~ *four*-headed muscle.
2. The trainer examined Cory's ~~triceps~~ *quadriceps*.
3. The trainer looked at Cory's quadriceps.

☆ Part 3

> A **prefix** comes before a base word. Below are some examples of **prefixes.**
>
> **untied   disobey   redraw**
>
> The prefixes **un-** and **dis-** often mean "not." The prefix **re-** may mean "again."

Indicate the word that correctly completes each sentence by filling in the circle.

1. It will be _unfair_ if we can't go to the party.
   ○ fair   ● unfair   ○ unright

2. If you _disconnect_ the television, it won't work.
   ○ reconnect   ● disconnect   ○ connect

3. Don't be afraid to _disagree_ if you have a good reason.
   ● disagree   ○ reagree   ○ unagree

4. Toby was _unsure_ of the formula.
   ○ dissure   ○ resure   ● unsure

5. Dad will _rebuild_ the shed.
   ● rebuild   ○ unbuild   ○ disbuild

Conventions of grammar, making inferences, prefixes
Directions: If necessary, read the directions for each part. When students have completed the page, present each item and the answer. Correct any errors

© 2001 SRA/McGraw-Hill. Permission is granted to reproduce for classroom use.

85

Part 4

Fill in each blank.

1. abdominal muscle
2. quadriceps
3. biceps
4. triceps
5. gastrocnemius
6. trapezius

Part 5

Use the rule to answer the questions.

> **The more milk you drink, the more vitamins you get.**

1. Aaron drinks four glasses of milk a week. Ed drinks six glasses of milk a week.
   a. Who gets more vitamins from milk? Ed
   b. How do you know? (Because Ed drinks more milk than Aaron)

2. Sandy drinks two gallons of milk a week. Cindy drinks three gallons of milk a week.
   a. Who gets more vitamins from milk? Cindy
   b. How do you know? (Because Cindy drinks more milk than Sandy)

Graphic aids, making inferences
Directions: If necessary, read the directions for each part. When students have completed the page, present each item and the answer. Correct any errors.

86

© 2001 SRA/McGraw-Hill. Permission is granted to reproduce for classroom use.

155

156

Name _____

Part 1

For each numbered word, write the letter of the word's definition.

1. obtain — e
2. mouth — g
3. criticize — f
4. reside — h
5. construct — a
6. residence — i
7. stomach — c
8. digestive system — d
9. residential — b
10. esophagus — j

a. (v.) build
b. (a.) that a place has many residences
c. (n.) the organ that mixes food with chemicals
d. (n.) the system that changes food into fuel for the body
e. (v.) get
f. (v.) find fault with
g. (n.) the part that takes in solid and liquid food
h. (v.) live somewhere
i. (n.) a place where someone resides
j. (n.) the tube that goes from the mouth to the stomach

Part 2

Make each statement mean the same thing as the statement in the box.

> The protective father constructed a stronger crib.

1. The father, who was protective, built a crib that would last longer.
2. The father, who constructed a stronger crib, was protective.
3. The protective father built a crib that was weaker. *stronger*
4. The careless father built a stronger crib. *protective*

Definitions, contradictions
Directions: If necessary, read the directions for each part. When students have completed the page, present each item and the answer. Correct any errors.

Name _____

Part 3

Write the number of the fact that explains why each thing happened.

1. Tina's triceps pulled.
2. Lisa's lower leg bone moved.

a. The muscle that pulled was in her upper arm. — 1
b. She pulled with a muscle that covered her femur. — 2
c. The muscle that pulled was in her leg. — 2

Part 4

Write **who** or **which** after each item.

1. His grandfather — who
2. Her table — which
3. My stomach — which
4. Her little brother — who
5. That woman — who
6. His humerus — which
7. Three bushes — which
8. A watermelon — which

☆ Part 5

> The prefixes **un-** and **dis-** often mean "not." The prefix **re-** often means "again."

Underline each word with a prefix. On the line write what the word means.

1. His shoelace is untied.
   not tied

2. My dog disobeys me sometimes.
   does not obey

3. Thomas will rebuild his engine.
   build again

4. This rock is unlike any I have ever seen.
   not like

5. Brian said that he disagrees with you.
   does not agree

6. I wish you would recopy your thank you letter.
   copy again

Drawing conclusions based on evidence, conventions of grammar, definitions/prefixes
Directions: If necessary, read the directions for each part. When students have completed the page, present each item and the answer. Correct any errors.

☆ Part 1

> The prefixes **un-** and **dis-** often mean "not." The prefix **re-** often means "again."

Complete each sentence by adding **un-**, **dis-**, or **re-** to the word in parentheses ( ).

1. Should I ___reheat___ your dinner?
   (heat)

2. The magician made the woman ___disappear___. (appear)

3. The man looked ___unconcerned___ about the accident. (concerned)

4. I want to ___reuse___ that wrapping paper. (use)

5. You have time to ___unpack___ your suitcase. (pack)

6. Will tried to ___discover___ where the water was coming in. (cover)

Part 2

Fill in each blank.

1. ___pelvis___
2. ___spine___
3. ___skull___
4. ___femur___
5. ___humerus___
6. ___ribs___

Prefixes, graphic aids
Directions: If necessary, read the directions for each part. When students have completed the page, present each item and the answer. Correct any errors.

Part 3

Write the number of the fact that explains why each thing happened.

1. Joe described a thing.
2. Frank told the action that things do.

a. He said a word like **learn.**   2
b. He said a verb.   2
c. He said an adjective.   1
d. He said a word like **simple.**   1

Part 4

Complete the instructions.

1. Draw a ___vertical___ line.

2. Draw a ___horizontal___ line at the ___top___ of the vertical line.

3. Draw a ___horizontal___ line at the ___bottom___ of the vertical line.

Part 5

Underline the common part. Then combine the sentences with **who** or **which.**

1. Noel is fascinated by her little sister.
   Her little sister is only six months old.
   <u>Noel is fascinated by her little sister, who is only six months old.</u>

2. Tim's father is calling for Tim.
   Tim is in the closet.
   <u>Tim's father is calling for Tim, who is in the closet.</u>

3. He hurt his triceps.
   His triceps covers his humerus.
   <u>He hurt his triceps, which covers his humerus.</u>

4. The little girl obtained those marbles.
   Those marbles are blue.
   <u>The little girl obtained those marbles, which are blue.</u>

Drawing conclusions based on evidence, following directions, conventions of grammar/writing sentences
Directions: If necessary, read the directions for each part. When students have completed the page, present each item and the answer. Correct any errors.

LESSON 50 — Name

Part 1

Write **R** for each fact that is **relevant** to what happened. Write **I** for each fact that is **irrelevant** to what happened.

The cat scratched the plumber.

1. The cat had black stripes. I
2. The plumber is thirty years old. I
3. The plumber yelled at the cat before the cat scratched him. R
4. The cat did not like people. R

Part 2

Write the conclusion of each deduction.

1. Most people have hair.
Dennis is a person.
So, maybe Dennis has hair.

2. Muscles do not move the bones they cover.
A quadriceps is a muscle.
So, a quadriceps does not move the bone it covers.

3. Fish breathe under water.
A carp is a fish.
So, a carp breathes under water.

Part 3

Fill in each blank with the word that has the same meaning as the word or words under the blank.

1. A groundhog _resides_ in our backyard. (lives)
2. Selma was able to _obtain_ food for her dog from the store. (get)
3. _Criticism_ can be helpful. (statements that criticize)
4. Terry _selected_ Duane for his team. (chose)

Part 4

Underline the nouns. Draw a line over the adjectives. Circle the verbs.

1. The man hurt his left quadriceps during the race.
2. The humerus is in the upper arm.
3. The digestive system includes many organs.
4. That woman selects colorful uniforms for the teams in our league.

Main idea/relevant and irrelevant details, deductions, vocabulary, conventions of grammar
Directions: If necessary, read the directions for each part. When students have completed the page, present each item and the answer. Correct any errors.

© 2001 SRA/McGraw-Hill. Permission is granted to reproduce for classroom use.

91

LESSON 50 — Name

☆ Part 5

A **suffix** is added at the end of a word.

thankful   enjoyment   quickly

The suffix **–ful** often means "full of."
The suffix **–less** often means "without."
The suffix **–er** often means "one who does."
The suffix **–ment** often means "the act of."

Underline each word that has a suffix. Fill in the circle next to the phrase that describes what the word means.

1. The builder bought nails and screws to construct a house.
○ one who buys   ● one who builds
2. Be careful when you play with the puppy.
● full of care   ○ full of play
3. It looked hopeless for my baseball team when we were down nine runs.
○ without runs   ● without hope
4. The paintings in the museum were beautiful.
● full of beauty   ○ full of paint

Part 6

Underline the common part. Then combine the sentences with **who** or **which**.

1. Doing pull-ups hardens your biceps.
Your biceps are part of your upper arms.
Doing pull-ups hardens your biceps, which are part of your upper arms.

2. The girl drinks milk.
Milk is good for her.
The girl drinks milk, which is good for her.

3. Everyone is born with soft bones.
Soft bones harden as we grow.
Everyone is born with soft bones, which harden as we grow.

4. Everyone has hair.
Hair helps trap body heat.
Everyone has hair, which helps trap body heat.

Suffixes, conventions of grammar/writing sentences
Directions: If necessary, read the directions for each part. When students have completed the page, present each item and the answer. Correct any errors.

92

© 2001 SRA/McGraw-Hill. Permission is granted to reproduce for classroom use.

Part 1

Cross out the words that are in the rule and the conclusion. Write the middle part.

1. Pat examined some bones.
   ~~A rib is a bone.~~
   So, maybe Pat examined a rib.

2. ~~Nouns do not tell how many.~~
   Construction is a noun.
   So, ~~construction does not tell how many.~~

3. ~~Some plants can grow without direct sunlight.~~
   Moss is a plant.
   So, maybe moss can grow without direct sunlight.

Part 2

Write **R** for each fact that is **relevant** to what happened. Write **I** for each fact that is **irrelevant** to what happened.

The man honked his horn.	
1. He was wearing a baseball cap.	I
2. He was angry with the driver in front of him.	R
3. He had a blue truck.	I
4. He liked to be loud.	R

Part 3

Fill in each blank.

1. esophagus
2. stomach
3. small intestine
4. liver
5. mouth
6. large intestine

Part 4

Underline the common part. Then combine the sentences with **who** or **which.**

1. Kerry selected some flowers for Carly.
   Carly is sick.
   Kerry selected some flowers for Carly, who is sick.

2. Two men constructed that dog house.
   That dog house is hidden by trees.
   Two men constructed that dog house, which is hidden by trees.

3. Six tall boys play ball on that court.
   That court has regulation basketball hoops.
   Six tall boys play ball on that court, which has regulation basketball hoops.

4. Their Doberman protects their house.
   Their house contains many valuables.
   Their Doberman protects their house, which contains many valuables.

☆ Part 5

Using the box below, add a suffix to each word. Tell what the new word means.

-ful	-er	-ment

1. fear
   Word: fearful
   Meaning: full of fear

2. work
   Word: worker
   Meaning: One who works

3. cheer
   Word: cheerful
   Meaning: full of cheer

4. enjoy
   Word: enjoyment
   Meaning: The act of enjoying

5. help
   Word: helpful
   Meaning: full of help

6. hope
   Word: hopeful
   Meaning: full of hope

LESSON 52   Name _____

Part 1

Write what each analogy tells.

- What ending each word has
- What part of speech each word is
- What each word means
- What verb each word comes from

1. Constructive is to **adjective** as **prediction** is to **noun**.

What part of speech each word is

2. Constructive is to **construct** as **prediction** is to **predict**.

What verb each word comes from

3. Constructive is to **ive** as **prediction** is to **ion**.

What ending each word has

☆ Part 2

Using the words in the box complete the sentences below.

| tireless | careful | successful |
| spoonful | quickly | teacher |

1. Please be __careful__ when you open the door.

2. My __teacher__ says that I am a good writer.

3. Try a __spoonful__ of custard.

4. Being __successful__ takes a lot of hard work and dedication.

5. I ran home __quickly__ before the rain started.

6. She is __tireless__ when it comes to practicing for her recital.

Analogies, suffixes
Directions: If necessary, read the directions for each part. When students have completed the page, present each item and the answer. Correct any errors.

© 2001 SRA/McGraw-Hill. Permission is granted to reproduce for classroom use.

LESSON 52   Name _____

Part 3

Make each contradiction true.

| It is hard to predict what shoppers will select. |

1. It is not easy to say what selections shoppers will make. hard

2. It is easy to make predictions about what shoppers will choose.

3. It is hard to say what shoppers will choose. hard

4. Saying what shoppers will choose is easy.

Part 4

| The predictable ending to the book left Anton unsatisfied. |

1. Underline the words that tell what what left Anton unsatisfied.

2. Draw a line over the words that tell what the book did.

3. Draw a box over the words that tell what kind of ending.

Part 5

Read the story and answer the questions. Circle the **W** if the question is answered by words in the story, and underline those words. Circle the **D** if the question is answered by a deduction.

> After naming their boat *The Twayne*, Terry and Wayne prepared to launch it into the pond. They laid pipes parallel to the shoreline, then rolled the boat over them to the water. One pipe rolled into the pond, but the boat made it safely into the water.
>
> Wayne took a piece of rope that was already tied to the boat and tied it to a stump on the shore so the boat wouldn't drift away. "Now we can sail whenever we want," Terry said.
>
> Wayne nodded. "We should only go out together, though," he said. "That way, we can watch out for each other."

1. Why will Terry and Wayne lay pipes parallel to the shoreline?

To roll the boat into the pond

W **D**

2. Why will Terry and Wayne only take the boat out together?

So they can watch out for each other.

W D

Contradictions, following directions, deductions
Directions: If necessary, read the directions for each part. When students have completed the page, present each item and the answer. Correct any errors.

© 2001 SRA/McGraw-Hill. Permission is granted to reproduce for classroom use.

Part 1

For each numbered word, write the letter of the word's definition.

1. criticize   _h_   a. (v.) guard
2. arteries   _k_   b. (n.) the very small tubes that connect arteries and veins
3. heart   _l_   c. (n.) the tubes that carry blood back to the heart
4. capillaries   _b_   d. (a.) careful about selecting things
5. predictable   _j_   e. (n.) the body system that moves blood around the body
6. protect   _a_   f. (n.) a statement that criticizes
7. circulatory system   _e_   g. (n.) a statement that predicts
8. selective   _d_   h. (v.) find fault with
9. prediction   _g_   i. (v.) look at
10. veins   _c_   j. (a.) that something is easy to predict
11. criticism   _f_   k. (n.) the tubes that carry blood away from the heart
12. examine   _i_   l. (n.) the pump that moves the blood

Definitions
Directions: If necessary, read the directions for each part. When students have completed the page, present each item and the answer. Correct any errors.

☆ Part 2

Many words have more than one meaning. Example:
Please be *patient* while we wait for the bus.
He was the doctor's first *patient* today.

To tell which meaning is being used:
- Look at the rest of the sentence.
- Decide which meaning of the word makes the most sense in the sentence.

Look at the underlined word in each sentence. Fill in the circle next to the meaning of the word that fits the sentence.

1. Mom asked him to turn on the outside <u>light</u>.
   - ● something by which we see
   - ○ not heavy

2. The animal was <u>light</u> enough to jump onto a thin branch.
   - ○ something by which we see
   - ● not heavy

3. I heard the dog <u>bark</u> at the squirrel.
   - ○ hard outside covering of a tree
   - ● the sound a dog makes

4. The <u>bark</u> of the tree was dark brown.
   - ● hard outside covering of a tree
   - ○ the sound a dog makes

Part 3

Write **R** for each fact that is **relevant** to what happened. Write **I** for each fact that is **irrelevant** to what happened.

> **Karen ate a big dinner last night.**

1. She didn't like to exercise.   _I_
2. She had not eaten since breakfast.   _R_
3. She sat next to her brother at the table.   _I_
4. She had heard her stomach rumbling all day.   _R_

Part 4

Underline the nouns. Draw a line over the adjectives. Circle the verbs.

1. Her brother (criticized) the short movie.
2. The pond (had) many birds and many mosquitoes.
3. Airplanes (were flying) in the clear sky.
4. The football player (predicted) the final score.
5. These three musicians (played) those CDs.

Multiple-meaning words, main idea/relevant and irrelevant details, conventions of grammar
Directions: If necessary, read the directions for each part. When students have completed the page, present each item and the answer. Correct any errors.

LESSON 54

Name _____

Part 1

Read the story and answer the questions. Circle the **W** if the question is answered by words in the story, and underline those words. Circle the **D** if the question is answered by a deduction.

> One day during the summer, Terry wanted to take the boat out on the pond. However, Wayne was at a lesson. Terry remembered that Wayne had said they should always take the boat out together. That way, they could help each other if there was a problem. Terry didn't want to wait for Wayne, though, so he pulled the rope off the stump and got in the boat. He sailed out to the middle of the pond. Without Wayne, he had a difficult time steering the boat. After twenty minutes of struggling with the boat, Terry headed for shore. He jumped out of the boat. "I think I'll go see if Wayne is home yet," he said.

1. What did Terry want to do at the beginning of the story?
   Take the boat out on the pond   (W) D

2. Why did Wayne think he and Terry should only use the boat together?
   So they could help each other
   if there was a problem   (W) D

3. What will Terry tell Wayne?
   (He couldn't steer the boat)   W (D)

Part 2

Cross out the words that are in the rule and the conclusion. Then write the middle part.

1. Cats ~~do not have gills.~~
   Princess is a cat.

   So, Princess ~~does not have gills.~~

2. Every one-syllable word ~~has a vowel.~~
   Brought is a one-syllable word.

   So, **brought** ~~has a vowel.~~

3. Howard ~~has~~ every kind of tool.
   A wrench is a tool.

   So, Howard ~~has a wrench.~~

4. All humans ~~have a heart.~~
   Leon is a human.

   So, Leon ~~has a heart.~~

Making inferences, writing deductions
Directions: If necessary, read the directions for each part. When students have completed the page, present each item and the answer. Correct any errors.

© 2001 SRA/McGraw-Hill. Permission is granted to reproduce for classroom use.

LESSON 54

Name _____

Part 3

Write **R** for each fact that is **relevant** to what happened. Write **I** for each fact that is **irrelevant** to what happened.

> **There were crows in the cornfield.**

1. There was a road next to the field.   I
2. There wasn't a scarecrow.   R
3. The corn was ready to be picked.   R
4. It was sunny.   I

Part 4

Make each statement mean the same thing as the statement in the box.

> **People praised Stuart for his car.**

1. Stuart was ~~criticized~~ praised for his automobile.
2. People were unable to find fault with Stuart's car.   praised
3. Stuart was ~~laughed at~~ praised for his car.
4. People complimented Stuart on his automobile.

☆ Part 5

Read each sentence below, noting the underlined word. Then, fill in the circle next to the definition that best matches the meaning of the underlined word.

1. The slice of bread had strawberry <u>jam</u> on it.
   ○ a difficult problem
   ● a spread made of fruit and sugar
   ○ to push or squeeze together

2. From the plane, Terry saw her aunt <u>wave</u> good-bye.
   ○ to sway
   ○ a moving ridge of water
   ● to move the hand in signal

3. The boy lost his turn because he didn't play <u>fair</u>.
   ● following the rules
   ○ sunny
   ○ treating everyone alike

4. Kim skinned his knee on the rough <u>bark</u> of the log.
   ○ to speak in a mean, loud manner
   ○ a sound that a dog makes
   ● the outside covering of a tree trunk

Main idea/relevant and irrelevant details, making inferences, multiple-meaning words
Directions: If necessary, read the directions for each part. When students have completed the page, present each item and the answer. Correct any errors.

100   © 2001 SRA/McGraw-Hill. Permission is granted to reproduce for classroom use.

☆ Part 1

Fill in the circle next to the correct meaning for each underlined word.

1. The rain continued to <u>beat</u> against the house.
   - ○ to mix
   - ● strike over and over

2. A <u>tear</u> rolled down the baby's cheek.
   - ● salty liquid from the eye
   - ○ rip or pull apart

3. Suddenly, the warning <u>bell</u> began to <u>ring</u>.
   - ○ narrow circle of metal worn on the finger
   - ● make the sound of a bell

4. The <u>racket</u> outside makes it hard to hear.
   - ● loud noise
   - ○ light bat used in sports

Part 2

Write the number of the fact that explains why each thing happened.

1. A dog ran through the residence.
2. A dog ran through the park.

a. The dog scared some geese.   2
b. The dog tracked mud inside.   1
c. The dog knocked over a lamp.   1
d. The dog splashed through a pond. 2

Part 3

Write **R** for each fact that is **relevant** to what happened. Write **I** for each fact that is **irrelevant** to what happened.

Gale rode his bike to school.

1. He went to bed late.   I
2. He liked riding his bike.   R
3. He had a lot of homework.   I
4. He lived a few blocks from school.   R
5. He had a new mountain bike.   R

Multiple-meaning words, drawing conclusions based on evidence, main idea/relevant and irrelevant details
Directions: If necessary, read the directions for each part. When students have completed the page, present each item and the answer. Correct any error

101

Part 4

Fill in the circle next to the word that has the same meaning as the word or words under the blank.

1. The doctor is _____ him for
   (finding fault with)
   eating unhealthful food.
   - ● criticizing ○ praising ○ warning

2. She _____ on the west side
   (lives)
   of town.
   - ○ stays ● resides ○ works

3. If you have a good knowledge of the teams, you might be able to _____ (say that it will happen)
   which will win.
   - ○ decide ○ guarantee ● predict

4. Dogs are used to _____ (guard)
   many homes.
   - ○ amuse ● protect ○ chase

Vocabulary
Directions: If necessary, read the directions for each part. When students have completed the page, present each item and the answer. Correct any errors.

102

164

☆ Part 1

Some nouns have irregular plural forms. These do not follow a pattern. Here are some examples:

woman   women / tooth   teeth

Write the plural form of each of the following nouns.

1. foot   <u>feet</u>
2. child   <u>children</u>
3. mouse   <u>mice</u>
4. man   <u>men</u>
5. ox   <u>oxen</u>
6. goose   <u>geese</u>

Write the singular form for each of the following plural forms.

7. children   <u>child</u>
8. oxen   <u>ox</u>
9. women   <u>woman</u>
10. teeth   <u>tooth</u>

Irregular plurals, conventions of grammar/writing sentences
Directions: If necessary, read the directions for each part. When students have completed the page, present each item and the answer. Correct any errors.

Part 2

Underline the common part. Fill in the circle next to the word that will combine the sentences correctly. Combine the sentences with that word.

1. The dentist examined the teeth.
   The teeth were rotten.
   ○ and   ● which   ○ who
   <u>The dentist examined the teeth,</u>
   <u>which were rotten.</u>

2. The CD was old.
   Cindy sold the CD.
   ○ and   ● which   ○ who
   <u>Cindy sold the CD, which was old.</u>

3. The players were frustrated.
   The referee was frustrated.
   ● and   ○ which   ○ who
   <u>The players and the referee</u>
   <u>were frustrated.</u>

4. Warren tore down the old birdbath.
   Warren tore down the old shed.
   ● and   ○ which   ○ who
   <u>Warren tore down the old birdbath</u>
   <u>and shed.</u>

Part 3

Write the middle part of each deduction.

1. Kyle did not look at any simians.
   <u>A monkey is a simian.</u>
   So, Kyle didn't look at any monkeys.

2. Burning things need oxygen.
   <u>Fires are burning things.</u>
   So, fires need oxygen.

Part 4

Complete the instructions.

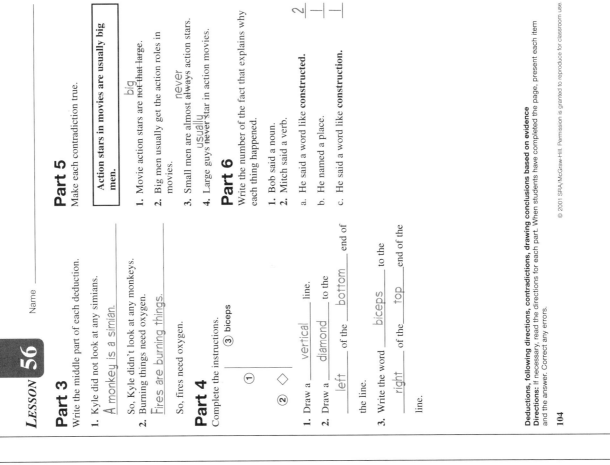

1. Draw a <u>vertical</u> line.
2. Draw a <u>diamond</u> to the <u>bottom</u> end of the line.
3. Write the word <u>biceps</u> to the <u>left</u> of the <u>bottom</u> end of the line.

Part 5

Make each contradiction true.

> **Action stars in movies are usually big men.**

1. Movie action stars are not that large.   *big*
2. Big men usually get the action roles in movies.
3. Small men are almost always action stars.   *never*
4. Large guys never star in action movies.   *usually*

Part 6

Write the number of the fact that explains why each thing happened.

1. Bob said a noun.
2. Mitch said a verb.

a. He said a word like **constructed.**   <u>2</u>
b. He named a place.   <u>—</u>
c. He said a word like **construction.**   <u>1</u>

Deductions, following directions, contradictions, drawing conclusions based on evidence
Directions: If necessary, read the directions for each part. When students have completed the page, present each item and the answer. Correct any errors.

☆ Part 1

A few nouns have the same singular and plural form.

Singular	Plural
deer	deer
moose	moose
sheep	sheep
reindeer	reindeer

Read each sentence. Underline the correct plural form of the word in parentheses.

1. It took three (mans, <u>men</u>) to move the piano.

2. The (oxes, <u>oxen</u>) pulled the heavy wagons.

3. The boy lost two (<u>teeth</u>, tooths) at lunch.

4. My (<u>feet</u>, foots) are swollen.

5. The (<u>mice</u>, mouses) ran under the bed.

6. Did the (childs, <u>children</u>) go to bed?

7. We saw the (deers, <u>deer</u>) in the forest.

8. The (<u>women</u>, womans) were planning a vacation.

9. All the (sheeps, <u>sheep</u>) were in the barn.

10. Two (moose, mooses) stood by the water tower.

Part 2

Tell which fact each statement contradicts.

1. Some dogs cannot bark.
2. All dogs have four legs.

a. Every dog barks at night.   1

b. That dog ran on two legs.   2

c. All dogs bark at people they do not know.   1

d. All border collies have only three legs.   2

Part 3

Write the middle part of the deduction.

1. Most years have 365 days.
   <u>2002 is a year.</u>
   So, maybe 2002 has 365 days.

2. Nouns do not tell what things do.
   <u>Selection is a noun.</u>
   So, **selection** does not tell what things do.

3. Some vehicles have pistons.
   <u>A jet is a vehicle.</u>
   So, maybe a jet has pistons.

Part 4

Complete the instructions.

1. Draw a <u>horizontal</u> <u>line</u>.

2. Draw a line that <u>slants</u> <u>down</u> to <u>the</u> left end of the <u>horizontal</u>.

3. Draw a line that <u>slants</u> <u>up</u> to <u>the</u> left end of the <u>horizontal</u> line.

Part 5

Underline the common part. Fill in the circle next to the word that combines the sentences correctly. Combine the sentences with that word.

1. That man works <u>at a bakery</u>.
   His son works <u>at a bakery</u>.
   ● and   ○ who   ○ which
   <u>That man and his son work</u>
   <u>at a bakery.</u>

2. The case protected <u>the CD</u>.
   <u>The CD</u> contained his favorite song.
   ○ and   ○ who   ● which
   <u>The case protected the CD</u>
   <u>which contained his favorite song.</u>

3. <u>Tom</u> has red hair.
   <u>Christina</u> has red hair.
   ● and   ○ who   ○ which
   <u>Tom and Christina have red hair.</u>

165

LESSON 58

Name _____

Part 1

For each numbered word, write the letter of the word's definition.

1. critical	_i_	a. (a.) helps to explain what happened
2. construct	_d_	b. (a.) does not help to explain what happened
3. relevant	_a_	c. (n.) the organ that gives food to the blood
4. liver	_h_	d. (v.) build
5. reside	_f_	e. (n.) the organ that stores food the body cannot use
6. constructive	_g_	f. (v.) live somewhere
7. large intestine	_e_	g. (a.) that something is helpful
8. irrelevant	_b_	h. (n.) the organ that makes chemicals to break down food
9. muscular system	_j_	i. (a.) that something criticizes
10. small intestine	_c_	j. (n.) the body system of muscles

☆ Part 2

Read the following sentences. Write the correct plural form above each underlined word.

    women   children   moose sheep ~~mooses~~ and ~~sheeps~~. feet

The ~~womans~~ took the ~~childs~~ to the zoo. There they saw ~~mooses~~ and ~~sheeps~~. While they were

                  teeth   children   feet

eating their lunches, a girl lost two ~~teeths~~. Before leaving, all of the ~~childs~~ put their ~~feets~~ in the

fountain.

Definitions, irregular plurals
Directions: If necessary, read the directions for each part. When students have completed the page, present each item and the answer. Correct any errors.
© 2001 SRA/McGraw-Hill. Permission is granted to reproduce for classroom use.

LESSON 58

Name _____

Part 3

Underline the common part. Fill in the circle next to the word that combines the sentences correctly. Combine the sentences with that word.

1. Doug likes going to concerts with <u>Tom</u>.
<u>Tom</u> enjoys a good show.
○ and ● who ○ which
Doug likes going to a concert with Tom, who enjoys a good show.

2. <u>Football</u> is a hard game.
<u>Football</u> requires a lot of concentration.
○ and ○ who ● which
Football is a hard game, which requires a lot of concentration.

3. <u>Dogs</u> like to run.
<u>Dogs</u> like to chew.
● and ○ who ○ which
Dogs like to run and chew.

Part 4

Read the story and answer the questions. Circle the **W** if the question is answered by words in the story, and underline those words. Circle the **D** if the question is answered by a deduction.

> After Wayne got back from his music lesson, he and Terry walked to the pond. When they reached the shore, they saw that the boat had drifted into the middle of the pond. "Oh, no, I forgot to tie up the boat," Terry moaned. He looked at Wayne, who just smiled.
> "These things happen," Wayne said. "Now we have to figure out how to get the boat back to shore."
> Terry asked, "Are we going to have to swim to the boat?"
> Wayne nodded. "It sure looks far away," Terry said.
> Wayne said, "We'll wear life jackets to be safe, in case we get tired." Wayne threw his arm over his brother's shoulder and said, "Let's get ready."

1. Why did Terry think he had forgotten to tie up the boat?
(Because it had drifted away from shore)   **W** Ⓓ

2. Did Wayne get mad at his brother for not tying up the boat? _No_   **W** Ⓓ

3. How were the boys going to get ready at the end of the story? <u>Get life jackets.</u>   Ⓦ **D**

Conventions of grammar/writing sentences, deductions
Directions: If necessary, read the directions for each part. When students have completed the page, present each item and the answer. Correct any errors.
108
© 2001 SRA/McGraw-Hill. Permission is granted for classroom use.

Name _____

☆ Part 1

Below are some words that tell the **time,** or when things happen.

today; this morning; once upon a time

Below are some words that tell the **order** in which things happen.

first, then, finally

Read the sentences. Underline every **time** or **order** word in each sentence.

1. Who went first to get ice cream?

2. Once upon a time, the trolls ruled the mountain.

3. I went to the doctor yesterday.

4. If we clean up the yard first, we can play basketball later.

5. They launched a space shuttle this morning.

6. My magazine finally came in the mail.

7. Dad had to go to New York today.

8. What was the last thing he told you before he left?

Part 2

Circle the subject.

1. (The old woman) went to the park.

2. (Two boys and a girl) sat on the curb.

3. (My three sisters) swim well.

4. (The dog) sat alone under the tree.

5. (She) ran through the park.

6. (Ted's dad) was happy it was after 3:00.

7. (The soccer ball) rolled into the net.

8. (The car) skidded off the road.

9. (The clouds) looked like animals.

10. (The clowns) are in the car.

Part 3

Write **R** for each fact that is **relevant** to what happened. Write **I** for each fact that is **irrelevant** to what happened.

Kendall's bike had a flat tire.

1. The bike had a new seat.   __I__

2. There was a nail in the tire.   __R__

3. She was so mad that she kicked the bike.   __I__

Sequence signal words, conventions of grammar, main idea/relevant and irrelevant details
Directions: If necessary, read the directions for each part. When students have completed the page, present each item and the answer. Correct any errors.
© 2001 SRA/McGraw-Hill. Permission is granted to reproduce for classroom use.

109

Name _____

Part 4

Write **bronchial tubes, trachea,** or **lungs** in each blank.

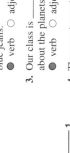
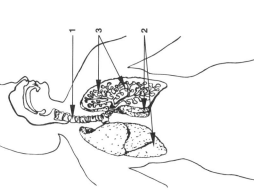

1. trachea

2. lungs

3. bronchial tubes

Part 5

Write a word that comes from **produce** in each blank. Then fill in the circle next to **verb, adjective,** or **noun.**

1. The Egyptians are a very _productive_ people.
   ○ verb   ● adjective   ○ noun

2. That company once _produced_ blue jeans.
   ● verb   ○ adjective   ○ noun

3. Our class is _producing_ a display about the planets.
   ● verb   ○ adjective   ○ noun

4. The report says that car _production_ went down last month.
   ○ verb   ○ adjective   ● noun

Graphic aids, conventions of grammar
Directions: If necessary, read the directions for each part. When students have completed the page, present each item and the answer. Correct any errors.
© 2001 SRA/McGraw-Hill. Permission is granted to reproduce for classroom use.

110

LESSON 60 Name _____

Part 1

Circle the subject.

1. (He) has big muscles in his arms.
2. (Those trees, bushes, and flowers) look great.
3. (This bagel) is chewy and tasty.
4. (People) like to sing along with the band at concerts.
5. (Horace and his brother) like to read scary books.
6. (Cordless telephones) are very useful.

Part 2

Write **R** for each fact that is **relevant** to what happened. Write **I** for each fact that is **irrelevant** to what happened.

> The man constructed a house.

1. He needed a place to live.   R
2. His hair was red.   I
3. He couldn't afford to hire someone.   R
4. He likes to swim.   I

Conventions of grammar, main idea/relevant and irrelevant details, sequence signal words
Directions: If necessary, read the directions for each part. When students have completed the page, present each item and the answer. Correct any errors.

© 2001 SRA/McGraw-Hill. Permission is granted to reproduce for classroom use.

LESSON 60 Name _____

☆ Part 3

Read each sentence. Underline the **time** and **order** words in each sentence. Then, write **time** if it is a time word or **order** if it is an order word.

1. This afternoon, I rode my bike.
   Time
2. First, I changed my clothes.
   Order
3. Then, I went to the garage.
   Order
4. Finally, I got on my bike.
   Order
5. I rode to my friend's house, then to the school. Order
6. After I got home, it was time for dinner.
   Order
7. Then, my brother and I did the dishes.
   Order
8. Tomorrow I will ride my bike again.
   Time

Part 4

Underline the common part. Fill in the circle next to the word that combines the sentences correctly. Combine the sentences with that word.

1. He examined her test.
   He gave her an A.
   ● and ○ who ○ which
   He examined her test and
   gave her an A.

2. The raccoon was alone.
   The garbage can was tipped over by the raccoon.
   ○ and ○ who ● which
   The garbage can was tipped over
   by the raccoon, which was alone.

3. The football team drank lots of water.
   Their coach drank lots of water.
   ● and ○ who ○ which
   The football team and their coach
   drank lots of water.

Part 5

Write what each analogy tells.

- What ending each word has
- What part of speech each word is
- What verb each word comes from
- What each word means

1. **Obtainable** is to **adjective** as **prediction** is to **noun.**
   What part of speech each word is

2. **Obtainable** is to **obtain** as **prediction** is to **predict.**
   What verb each word comes from

3. **Obtainable** is to **that something can be obtained** as **prediction** is to **a statement that predicts.**
   What each word means

Conventions of grammar/writing sentences, analogies
Directions: If necessary, read the directions for each part. When students have completed the page, present each item and the answer. Correct any errors.

© 2001 SRA/McGraw-Hill. Permission is granted to reproduce for classroom use.